Praying for Others

Thomas D. Elliff

BROADMAN PRESS
Nashville, Tennessee

The letter in chapter 10 is from *Behind the Ranges* by Mrs. Howard Taylor. Copyright 1964 by The Moody Bible Institute of Chicago. Used by permission of Overseas Missionary Fellowship, China Inland Missions.

Scripture quotations marked RSV are from the Revised Standard Version of the Bible, copyrighted 1946, 1952, © 1971, 1973.

Dewey Decimal Classification: 248.3
Subject Heading: PRAYER
Library of Congress Catalog Card Number: 79-52341

Printed in the United States of America.

To Jeannie
in appreciation for her constant encouragement
to walk in the light of Bible promises

Contents

1
The Practice of Prayer

Consider for a moment the following questions: Why is it that we think and do so little of what our Lord thinks and does so much? I am thinking now specifically of the practice of prayer. What has happened to the practice of prayer? It appears that of all the disciplines of the Christian life it is the most neglected.

Such was not the case in the earthly life of our Lord. Those brief years are punctuated with prayer. The greater the task, the greater the intensity with which he prayed. On some occasions he quietly slipped away to the place of communion with the Father. At other times the tremendous burdens of his ministry required that he send his followers away that he might gain precious moments of prayer. He prayed before the cross; on the cross; and after his resurrection. Our salvation rests upon the fact that "He ever liveth to make intercession" (Heb. 8:25). Little wonder that his followers begged him, "Lord, teach us to pray" (Luke 11:1).

The effect of prayer can easily be seen in the life of our Lord. Has it ever occurred to you that he never wasted a moment of time? To waste time would have been to sin. The practice of prayer enabled him to distinguish between those demands which were merely urgent and those ministries which were most important. Jesus wasted no words or motions because the priorities of his life were established through prayer.

What a contrast to the Christian who lives with the nagging awareness that he is accomplishing little that is worthwhile. Pushed around by pressing matters he feels like he is winning some battles but losing the war. Minutes, hours, days, and years seem to be wasted on matters which have little, if any, eternal significance.

What has happened to the practice of prayer in your life? The command to pray is not in question here. God's Word abounds with commands, examples, promises, and encouragements to pray. What is missing is the obedient heaven-bending, hell-binding practice of prayer.

Look at the commands and then look at your own experience. We are told, for instance, that we "ought always to pray and not to faint" (Luke 18:1). But we generally do not think of prayer until we faint. We have reduced prayer for the most part to a matter of etiquette. Encouraged to "pray without ceasing" (1Thess. 5:17), we carefully insure that our meetings never start or cease without praying. Designated "Weeks of Prayer" are too often weak in prayer. I imagine heaven's hosts bending toward earth at the announcement of a "time of prayer," and hearing nothing more than the "whine of prayer" chorused by an assembly of defeated Christians who have forgotten the admonition: "Ye have not, because ye ask not" (Jas. 4:2).

Take the measure of your own prayer life. Are you in danger of being called "camel-knees" as was James, our Lord's half-brother and pastor of the Jerusalem church? He was called "camel-knees" because of the callouses worn on his knees as a result of endless hours of prayer. Do you have the prayer confidence of George Mueller who sought God alone for the needs of thousands of orphans? Refusing to ask any man for anything, George Mueller's carefully kept diary chronicles God's daily, sometimes hourly, never-failing provisions.

Can you claim the *prayer consistency* of Hudson Taylor, founder of the great China Inland Mission. Those who traveled with him record that no matter how grueling the day you would hear the rustle behind his curtain and see the flickering candle as he rose a few hours past midnight to have his time with God. Have your years recorded the *prayer effectiveness* of praying John Hyde, missionary to India? While his ministry spanned only a few brief years, thousands were born into the kingdom on the prayers of a man who trusted God first for one, then two, then three, and before his death, four souls each day.

Do you know something of the *prayer energy* of David Brainerd? Sickly, weak, destined to live only a few years, he determined to share the light of the gospel with the Indians on the Eastern seaboard. Faithful in witness and toiling in prayer, sometimes praying through the hours in knee-deep snow, he was privileged to see one of the greatest movings of God in the history of the North American continent.

Several years ago I began to study the lives of great people of prayer. I read about the way God used men and women dedicated to the practice of prayer to change the course of history. The more I read the more convicted I became of my own prayerlessness. I had seen a certain measure of success in the pastorate and was considered by some to have arrived at a most enviable position. Now I had come, without benefit of human criticism or encouragement, under the searching eye of God. Alone before him I could not defend my utter lack of prayer.

It was not that I did not appear to be a man of prayer. A few well-chosen words were always available for any occasion. I preached about prayer, conducted prayer meetings, and always responded in the affirmative to those who asked, "Pastor, will you pray for me?" "I'll be praying for you" were the last words of every visit. And each letter closed with the assurance that the reader could "count on our continued prayers." But, if they took me seriously, I let them down. My personal prayer altar was broken down and deserted. Except for spasmodic periods of renewed effort, I just did not pray.

Now what would I do? I was at a loss. God had found me out. Or, rather, God was allowing me to find out about myself. It had not really disturbed me in times past. But now I felt as if my case had finally come up before the court of heaven. The evidence was in, and I was guilty of disobedience by gross negligence.

Unable to rest I settled on something like a "trial run." Looking back now, in the light of God's promises, it all seems rather foolish. But it was serious business then—and God took me seriously. I determined to spend the morning hours in my study in uninterrupted prayer. To some people that may not sound difficult. But to a pastor, who considered the ministry something like a public relations position, it was difficult. Think of all the coffee breaks, jokes, telephone calls, and fellowship I would miss, not to mention the seemingly endless list of administration responsibilities!

When the office door closed behind me Monday morning, I took my Bible, fell to my knees, and told the Lord an out-and-out lie. "Lord, you know how I have desired to have time alone with you in prayer." In less time than it takes to tell it, the Lord reminded me that, for the most part, we do what we want to do. I was forced to agree that I had not had the time for prayer because I had not taken the time to pray.

I confess that I frequently glanced at my watch during those first few minutes of prayer. Each minute seemed to take forever. I discovered that I was not really accustomed to communion with God. I felt uncomfortable as I framed the words, thinking how they would sound to others. Praying for all the usual people, events, and needs did not dispel the uneasiness I felt. It was obvious that God wanted to do business on a deeper level. He wanted to deal with my personal rebellion to his way. A greater barrier of unconfessed sin had to crumble under the forgiveness of God during the next few hours. Cleansed by the work of Jesus, according to 1 John 1:9, I could now see clearly the issues that confronted the members of my congregation. It was then I began to pray in earnest for them.

At noon I opened the door of my study. I discovered a stranger waiting to visit for "just a moment." "Pastor," he said, "You don't know me. I was just driving by the church and something

told me to come in here and ask you how I could get saved."
In a matter of minutes he was born into God's family. He then
rushed to meet his wife and led her to receive Christ. At noon
on the next two days similar experiences awaited me when I opened
the door of my study after a morning in prayer. In addition, it
seemed that God protected that time. Church members were
understanding of their pastor's desire to be available to God.

God dealt with me graciously as I spent more time with him.
During the next two weeks, over one hundred individuals walked
the aisle of our church during the invitation time. More than
one half of them desired to profess Christ as Lord and Savior.
In the events of those weeks God convinced me that he intends
prayer to be a vital tool in the Christian's walk and welfare.

It is my intent in the next few pages to share some of the
basic principles of prayer and, more specifically, to show how
these principles relate to praying for other people. Before reading
these chapters please take the measure of your prayer life. What
has happened to the practice of prayer in your life? What are
you willing to sacrifice in order to become a person of great prayer?

2
The Word of God and Prayer

It is significant that in God's economy the practice of prayer was never intended to be divorced from the practice of searching the Scriptures. Jesus said, "If you abide in me, and my words abide in you, ye shall ask what you will, and it shall be done unto you" (John 15:7). Effective prayer rests on the authority of God's will as revealed through his Word. God's Word is consistently opened to those who prayerfully appeal to him for discernment.

Sometimes I'm approached by individuals who desire to learn a new method or system for prayer or Bible study. Frustrated on both counts, they are longing for a new insight that will make them want to pray and search the Scriptures. There is no such gimmick. In the end these two practices must be seen as great, worthwhile, and indispensable disciplines of the Christian life. It can be said with certainty, however, that if you meet the Lord in the Scriptures you will long to commune with him in prayer. If you should meet the Lord in prayer, you will long to walk with him along Bible pathways.

As a young teenager I was privileged to hear E. F. "Preacher" Hallock of Norman, Oklahoma. My father was the pastor of our church and "Preacher" Hallock was the visiting evangelist. I can clearly remember my father sharing with the congregation that "Preacher" Hallock was something of an authority on prayer. It would be difficult for me to recall a great deal of what "Preacher" Hallock said that week. This one observation made a definite impression: "If I had to choose between reading the Bible and prayer, I would choose to read the Bible. It is more important for me to hear what God is saying than for God to hear what I am saying." Those words contain a strong warning to the folks for whom Bible study is less than a priority.

I heard "Preacher" Hallock speak again, this time at a week-long youth encampment. "Read God's Word and ask him to give you a Bible promise," he emphasized. "No matter what the situation, he has a word for you in his Word." My father gathered our family together and said, "This man is telling the truth. From now on our family will operate on the principle of Bible promises." Right then I accepted the principle without question. A few weeks later I prayerfully asked God to give me a Bible promise regarding my life's vocation. He answered through Isaiah 6:8 and called me into the gospel ministry. It was not until years later that I began to see just how important the Word of God is to the practice of prayer.

Understanding how the Bible relates to prayer requires a short history lesson. Man, as God created him, has the remarkable capacity to live in both the physical world and the spiritual world at the same time. So that man might live in this physical world, God has given him a body with five senses—seeing, hearing, smelling, tasting, and touching. All that we know about our physical environment we know on the basis of information received through these five senses.

Genesis 1:27 tells us that man was created in God's image. In John 4:24 Jesus emphasizes that God is a spirit. From this we know that man originally communicated with God on the spiritual level and with the world on a physical level. The first few chapters of Genesis indicate that, before falling into sin, Adam and Eve were as sensitive to the voice of God as they were to any of the physical sights or sounds in the Garden of Eden.

In addition to the body, with which he could communicate in the physical realm, and the spirit, with which he could commune with God, the Bible also speaks of the "soul" of man. By giving

Man is three parts in one: body, soul, and spirit (1 Thess. 5:23). With his body, he perceives physical phenomena through his five senses: seeing, hearing, tasting, smelling, and touching.

All this information goes to his soul, comprised of his intellect, emotions, and will.

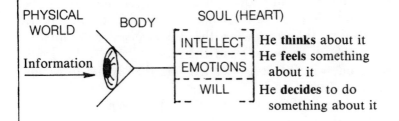

BUT

With his spirit he perceives spiritual phenomena through his spiritual senses. This information also goes to the soul.

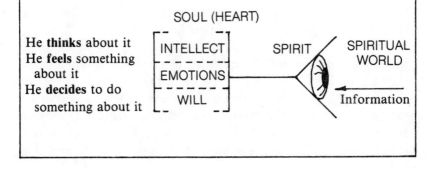

man a soul (also called the "heart" in some instances) God made it possible for man to choose to respond to God's Word or the world. With his soul (intellect, emotion, and will) he could weigh the information received by his body or his spirit and determine his course of action. God created man in this fashion so that a meaningful relationship of love and worship could exist between himself and mankind. Man's love and obedience would have meant little unless he had the option *not* to love and obey.

From the beginning Satan, the "prince of this world," has attempted to draw man's allegiance away from God. He appealed to the body ("the woman saw that the tree was good for food and pleasant to the eyes") and the soul ("a tree to be desired to make one wise") to convince Eve and then Adam to commit sin against God.

God had said, "Of the tree of the knowledge of good and evil; thou shalt not eat of it: for in the day that thou eatest thereof thou shalt surely die" (Gen. 2:17). When Adam and Eve took from the tree, they died—not in body or soul, but in spirit. They lost their capacity for fellowship with God—to perceive spiritual truths. Sin entered the human race and became the tendency of all men.

Because every man is sinful by nature (Rom. 3:23), he suffers the same kind of death experienced by Adam and Eve. He has lost his capacity to commune, or fellowship, with God. The apostle Paul uses the phrase "natural man" to describe the man who tends to make every decision solely on the basis of physical information and whatever logic or emotion he attaches to it. "But the natural man receiveth not the things of the Spirit of God: for they are foolishness unto him: neither can he know them, because they are spiritually discerned" (1 Cor. 2:14).

How can a man escape this enslavement to the natural world over which Satan is the prince? How can he establish fellowship and commune with God? His only hope is to be "born again" in the spirit. "That which is born of the flesh is flesh; and that which is born of the Spirit is spirit. Marvel not that I said unto thee, ye must be born again" (John 3:6-7). When a man is born again, the Holy Spirit enters his life and reestablishes that which was lost in the Garden of Eden.

The Christian can, if he will, hear God as readily as he hears what the world has to say. But the battle begun in the Garden of Eden is being waged with equal ferocity today. Satan assaults the Christian with information which contradicts the Word of God. Every Christian is called upon to decide what is true. Is truth what the world says? Or is truth what God's Word says?

The believer is quick to respond: "Truth is what God's Word says!" Unfortunately the confession of our lips is not often matched by the behavior of our lives. Bound for heaven we live as if we are bound to the earth—a condition properly described in 1 Corinthians 3 as a "carnal" or "fleshly" orientation.

When we come to God in prayer he frees us from earthly bondage and places heaven's resources at our disposal. As such, our prayer must be based upon the truths of God's Word. Jesus said, "If ye continue in my word, then are ye my disciples indeed; And ye shall know the truth, and the truth shall make you free" (John 8:31-32).

Nehemiah stands out in the history of God's people as a great man of prayer. Following a lengthy period of captivity the Israelites were allowed to return to Jerusalem and rebuild the Temple. For years afterward, however, the walls of the great city of God lay in rubble and disarray.

Under the leadership of Nehemiah and against seemingly insurmountable odds, God's people began to rebuild the walls. Nehemiah received opposition to this project from every corner. He was laughed at and scorned for his seeming foolishness. His integrity was challenged. Greed, discouragement, and persecution threatened the success of the project. Putting it simply, the world was saying, "It cannot be done."

On what basis could Nehemiah continue? He had searched

the Scriptures and prayed according to the promise of God! "Remember I beseech thee, the word that thou commanded at thy servant Moses, saying . . . I will gather them from thence and will bring them unto the place that I have chosen to set thy name" (Neh. 1:8-9).

Nehemiah did not question the validity of God's Word. He had determined that God's Word is true regardless of what the world says. That is a determination you must make if you are to pray effectively.

3
Faith and Prayer

The difficult part of prayer is not asking but believing. It's difficult to believe something you do not know. This is why in the preceding chapter you were asked to determine what constitutes truth or, to put it simply, what you will believe. Until you know something is true, you can "hope" but you cannot "believe." Faith is more than "hoping hard."

Faith is essential for effective prayer. The Word of God indicates that every aspect of our lives should operate by an exercise of faith. We are saved by faith (Eph. 2:8-9); we live by faith (Gal. 2:20); we walk by faith (2 Cor. 5:7); we stand by faith (1 Cor. 16:13); we overcome obstacles by faith (Matt. 17:20); we fight by faith (1 Tim. 6:12); we gain the victory by faith (1 John 5:4); all in addition to praying by faith (Matt. 21:22). "Without faith it is impossible to please him [God]," we read in Hebrews 11:6. The apostle Paul sums it up by saying, "Whatsoever is not of faith is sin" (Rom. 14:23).

It is obvious that God wants us to live in such a manner that to fail to believe is to fail completely. What is faith? What does it mean to "believe." We are permitted an insight into the nature of faith through the window of Hebrews 11:1-2. "Now faith is the substance of things hoped for, the evidence of things not seen. For by it the elders obtained a good report."

"The Substance of Things Hoped For"

The word *substance* in verse 1 may be accurately translated as "assurance." After all, we are assured of the reality of something when we see or feel the substance. Haven't we all said at one time or another, "Seeing is believing!"

Notice however that "faith is the substance of things *hoped for*." The verse does not say that faith is hope. It does indicate, however, than when our desires are in accord with God's will for us, he gives us faith—and that faith is a substance as real as anything we have ever touched! A paraphrase of this statement might read: **Faith is being assured that your desire is a reality, ready to be claimed.**

How does assurance come? It comes as God speaks by his Spirit through his Word. Often people repeatedly express their desires trying desperately to "work up" their faith. "I'm just believing he will be healed," I have heard people say of dying loved ones. Sometimes when death occurs, they are puzzled because they were under the impression they prayed with faith. Actually they prayed *hoping* rather than *believing* for they had not received the assurance from God's Word that their loved one would be healed. *Faith* in the biblical sense is based on the revelation of God's will through his Word.

This element of faith is illustrated in an interesting manner in the fifth chapter of John's Gospel. There was a man beside the pool of Bethesda who had suffered thirty-eight years with a crippling infirmity. Do you think he had ever tried to walk in all those years? Of course! How else did he discover he could not? Do you think he wanted to walk? Certainly! For years he had been brought to the pool waiting for the miraculous stirring of the water. Do you think he hoped one day to be able to walk? Yes! That is why he continued making repeated attempts to enter the pool at the proper moment. Do you think that after thirty-eight years he was convinced that, apart from a miracle, he would never walk? He seemed to have given up. "I have no friends," he complained.

Now suppose you had come upon this pitiful figure and asked, "Do you want to be made well?" He would have answered in the affirmative. And suppose you had said, "Then get up and walk!" You can be assured he would have felt you were having a laugh at his expense. After all, he couldn't walk.

But that is precisely how Christ handled the situation. When Christ said, "Rise, take up thy bed, and walk" (v. 9) faith was born in the heart of that man. Assured that his desire was a reality only waiting to be claimed he stood up and walked.

What was the basis of this man's faith? Not your word or mine. Not physical evidence or experience. From those vantage points nothing had changed. The assurance that his desire was a reality, ready to be claimed, came at the moment he heard the Word of the Lord. "Faith comes by hearing, and hearing by the word of God" (Rom. 10:17).

"The Evidence of Things Not Seen"

The word *evidence* may be properly translated here as a "conviction." It has been said that while a belief is something you hold, a conviction is something which holds you. You cannot shake loose from a conviction. A paraphrase of this statement might read as follows: **Faith is being convicted that something is real even though you cannot perceive it with your physical senses.** This is directly counter to the "seeing is believing" philosophy.

Suppose a college student, reared in the deep South, is attending his first semester of school in Alaska. He has taken his heaviest clothing, but obviously what is sufficient for the southern climate will not be enough to keep him warm in Alaska. Early in the year the hard, cold winter sets in. His parents, in a rush of concern, buy him an extra heavy coat and send it by mail. Then they call him to let him know he is to expect a package.

Standing in an outdoor phone booth, blue with the cold, the student receives his parents' phone call. His father says, "We have sent you a coat." How does his son reply? If he responded to his earthly father in the manner most of us respond to our heavenly Father, the son would continue to beg for the coat.

He might go on to state all the reasons for needing the coat. Additionally, he might make repeated phone calls to make sure his parents understand the need.

That is not his response. He simply says, "Thanks." Thanks for what? The coat, of course. He has not seen or felt the coat. But he has the assurance that it is real even though he cannot perceive it with his physical senses. That assurance has come to him by the word of his father.

His friends are mystified at his behavior. "Don't you need a coat?" they ask as he walks through the snow, blue with cold. "No!" he passes off their question, "I've got one!" Every Christian should have a life-style just as unexplainable in human terms. "Are you not worried?" they ask, assessing a certain need in the Christian's life. "No!" responds the Christian, "I have the answer." He does if he has the word of the Father.

"Be careful for nothing;" says the Word of God, "but in every thing by prayer and supplication with thanksgiving, let your requests be made known unto God" (Phil. 4:6). Thanksgiving is your faith response when you are convicted that the answer is real even though you cannot perceive it with your physical senses.

"By It the Elders Obtained a Good Report"

There are many possible interpretations of Hebrews 11:2. We can be assured that, whatever its meaning, it acknowledges the fact that many of the persons of the Old Testament were noted for their faith. This is especially interesting in light of the fact that the Hebrew language of the Old Testament did not really possess an adequate word for "faith."

The Greek language of the New Testament time expresses many abstract thoughts. A rainstorm, for instance, might be described as "tears expressing the sadness of one of their many gods or goddesses." The Hebrew language, on the contrary, spoke in real or concrete terms. Rain would be described as "water falling from the sky." For this reason, the Old Testament Hebrew language had no good word for faith because you could not see it. On the other hand, they did have a word for faithfulness, because you could see faithfulness.

It stands to reason that faith, in the biblical sense, is not something you think or feel, it is something you do. **Faith is acting on the revealed will of God.** As you go on to read the "Roll Call of Faith" in Hebrews 11, note that none of these individuals were noted for what they thought. **They were noted for their actions.**

Many people labor under the tragic misconception that faith is believing God can do anything. Of course he can! But mere acceptance of that fact is not "faith" in the biblical sense. Faith is acting on what God has revealed as his plan. God once told Moses to strike a rock so that he could provide water for Israel. Moses acted in faith, struck the rock, and God supplied their need. Later the children of Israel again complained for lack of water. God could have brought water from the rock again. Moses believed that and struck the rock in anger. That was not an act of faith for it was not according to God's revealed plan. This act of disobedience displeased the Lord and cost Moses his personal entrance into Canaan.

Faith Is . . .

. . . the assurance that your desire is a reality ready to be claimed.

. . . the conviction that something is real even though you cannot perceive it with your physical senses.

. . . acting on the revealed will of God.

When you have settled that God's Word is true regardless of what the world says, you are ready to believe. When you can believe . . . you are ready to pray.

4
Six Steps
to Praying with Success

There is a simplicity at the heart of the Christian life and its various elements which is often lost in its treatment by "technical specialists." The thoughts of this chapter, indeed the entire book, are offered with the prayer that the reader will not become more intrigued with a system than with this simple fact: "As you have therefore received Christ Jesus the Lord, so walk ye in him" (Col. 2:6). Those few words state the pattern of operation for every aspect of the Christian life, prayer not excepted.

Consider how we receive Jesus Christ the Lord. The circumstances of our entrance into the Christian life may differ widely. In their elemental aspects the experiences are identical. For that reason I am sure you can identify with the elements of my personal conversion. As a young boy there was first brought to my heart the awareness, call it conviction, that I needed fellowship with God—a fellowship which was impossible because of the presence of sin in my life. Since the issue was my relation to God, it was to him I turned for the answer. God, in turn, spoke to me by his Spirit through his Word. (In my particular case God accomplished this through a discussion with my parents.)

As a "preacher's kid" I am sure I had heard the great salvation verses on hundreds of previous occasions. But then, in the context of my need, God's Spirit brought those verses to life and I heard them and received them as personally spoken by God to me. Accepting God's Word as true, I made a faith request that Jesus would enter my heart, take away my sin, and be my Lord. I believed in him, and he, according to his promise, granted the

27

salvation which I now joyfully confess is mine.

God's Word simply states that the elemental pattern of my conversion should, in turn, be the elemental pattern for all the practices of my Christian life. On the following pages we will see how this pattern fits the practice of prayer. This pattern is comprised of six steps: (1) A God-acknowledged need enters my life; (2) I decide to turn to God for the answer; (3) God reveals his will by His Spirit and through his Word; (4) I discern and receive God's Word as true; (5) I make a faith request; and (6) God hears and answers.

A great prayer promise is found in 1 John 5:14-15. "And this is the confidence that we have in him, that, if we ask any thing according to his will, he heareth us: And if we know that he hears us, whatsoever we ask, we know that we have the petitions that we desired of him." It is stated that the key to answered prayer is asking according to the will of God. These six steps will help you to discover the will of God regarding any circumstances and to ask accordingly.

Step 1: A God-Acknowledged Need Enters My Life

Every believer must come to grips with the fact that he is intimately related to a God who is sovereign. However biblical, this is an especially difficult doctrine for those who would pit man's freedom against God's sovereignty and say that it must be one or the other. It must suffice that both doctrines are taught in the Scriptures; both doctrines stand true; and the fact that we cannot comprehend everything about the way God has chosen to operate does not erase their truth or hinder their operation.

The fact that God is sovereign means that some words are *not* a part of his vocabulary. God never says, "Oops!" or, "I didn't know that!" or, "That one sure slipped up on me!" To believe in a sovereign God you must agree that every circumstance of your life is known by God before it occurs and, for whatever reason, he does not alter its course.

"What about the problems caused by Satan?" you may protest. The book of Job alone is sufficient evidence that God is even the God of the devil. He is, indeed, a sovereign God and his sovereignty should be of great encouragement to the Christian for "all things work together for good to them that love God, to them who are the called according to his purpose" (Rom. 8:28).

Unfortunately, most Christians do not view their problems, or needs, in the proper perspective. Picture, for instance, a great need at the door of your life. (You may already have one in mind.) How do you respond? Do you cower and confess your fear? "I was afraid that would happen!" or "I am afraid of what will happen!" Confessions of this nature simply tell Satan how to get to you at the point of your weakness. Remember that after losing his health, wealth, family, and friends, Job lamented "the thing which I greatly feared is come upon me" (Job 3:25). Apparently Satan takes good notes when we confess our fears. Why do we speak and act as if there could arise a need larger than God's ability to meet that need?

Actually we should welcome difficulties and attach to them the following definitions:

• *My problem is actually a platform upon which God can prove to the world how powerfully he provides for his people.* The greater the need, the greater the testimony to God's grace and often, by God's design, the greater the audience.

• *My problem is a signal from God that he has available for me a blessing for which I have not asked.* He is actually letting me have this need so I will ask for and accept what he wants me to have.

• *My problem is an indication from God that he has not given up on the possibility I might learn how to pray.* I am repeatedly told in the Scriptures that God's provision comes in answer to prayer.

Think of it! The needs of your life right now are a part of

God's plan to set you praying. Make a list of your needs and show the world and the devil how powerful God is by attaching new meanings to your troubles.

Step 2: I Decide to Turn to God for the Answer . . . First

"Take it to the Lord in Prayer." That frequently stated advice is usually met with "Of course! I always do that!" Experience shows that for many Christians, God is the last resort.

Think about your usual procedure on encountering some need. "Shall I see another doctor?" "Perhaps I should contact my pastor." "Maybe my friend will have some advice." "I'll try to ignore the situation and maybe it will go away." "A good counselor will probably have the right answer." Finally, if none of these bring adequate assistance, "Dear God . . . Help!" It could be that God's answer for you might be found by seeking advice from a friend or allowing time to solve the difficulty. Why waste time pursuing any course of action until God has specifically directed you to do so?

We are reminded in Ephesians 6:12, that "we wrestle not against flesh and blood, but against principalities, against powers, against the rulers of the darkness of this world, against spiritual wickedness in high places." The Christian's walk and warfare is not merely a "flesh and blood" or physical issue. This is why the needs in your life should trigger an immediate consultation with the Lord. "Father, what is your will concerning this situation?" Determine to turn to God *now* for his answer to your needs.

Step 3: God Reveals His Will

The record of God's dealings with men reveals that he has spoken both "at sundry times and in divers manners" (Heb. 1:1). For this reason it would be foolish to say that God will always or only speak to us in a certain manner. On the other hand, the Bible clearly indicates the basic fashion by which we can trust him to reveal his will. He speaks (a) by his Spirit and (b) through his Word.

In 1 Corinthians 2:9-10,12 the apostle Paul emphasizes the role of the Holy Spirit in revealing the will of God. "But as it is written, Eye hath not seen, nor ear heard, neither have entered into the heart of man, the things which God has prepared for them that love him." Here he is making it clear that the will of God is not sensed by the body or "thought up" by man. He continues, however, by stating that "God has revealed them unto us by his Spirit; for the Spirit searches all things, yea the deep things of God." And finally he comes to this joyous conclusion, "Now we have received, not the spirit of the world, but the Spirit who is of God; *that we might know* the things that are freely given to us of God." (Emphasis mine.)

How does the Holy Spirit speak to the believer? God uses many methods of speaking to us. He has assured us that one way he will always speak to us is through his Word, the Bible. The apostle Paul was referring to that fact when he wrote to Timothy: "All scripture is given by inspiration [i.e. spirit breathed] of God, and is profitable for doctrine, for reproof, for correction, for instruction in righteousness, That the man of God may be perfect, thoroughly furnished unto all good works" (2 Tim. 3:16-17).

"*All* the Scripture," Paul is saying, "provides *all* a Christian needs to know to do *all* things right." In the context of your need the Holy Spirit lifts the printed word off the pages of Scripture, speaks them to your heart, and they become the living word.

The original language of the Scripture is useful to illustrate how God's Spirit speaks through his Word to reveal his will. "Logos" is the word used to describe an expression of thought such as those recorded on the printed page. "Rhema," on the other hand, is the word used to describe the spoken expression. For instance, in Ephesians 6:11-17 the Christian is told to take unto himself various pieces of armor for spiritual warfare. In verse 17 he is encouraged to fight with the "sword of the Spirit, which is the word of God." Here "rhema" is used for "word." Therefore it is "the sword of the Spirit which is the word God has spoken to you."

How exciting it is to know that God stands ready to reveal his will to me by his Spirit through his Word. There are some prerequisites to hearing what God is saying. We will examine them in the next step.

Step 4: I Discern and Receive God's Word as True

People must speak and listen in the same language if communication is to be adequate. It is the same in communicating with God. If God is speaking by his Spirit through his Word, *it is the individual, living in the fullness of the Spirit and engaged in a consistent study of the Word, who discerns God's will.*

Jesus said, "If you abide in me, and my words abide in you, ask what you will, and it shall be done for you" (John 15:7, RSV). To "abide in Christ" is to live in the fulness of the Spirit. It means, literally, to settle down, or make your home, entirely within the boundaries of Christ. Once again, this is the only place of Christian freedom since he is the "truth" (John 14:6). Abiding in Christ means having no rebellion in your heart toward the Lord or his will for your life. It means living in complete surrender to him.

Some Christians live as prisoners of war, feeling trapped against their will in an alien country behind the fences of an enemy who denies them their desires. This is not abiding, because the heart still rebels. When a Christian gladly acknowledges that he has changed his citizenship and joyfully subjects himself to his new Lord, he is "abiding in Christ."

Notice, however, that abiding in Christ is only the first step. Jesus also states that his words must abide in me. That is, the Bible must be at home in my life. This implies the necessity of consistent Bible study.

There is nothing sporadic about "abiding." Occasionally a desperate brother throws open his Bible, jams his finger into the page, and receives light from a verse he finds there. This is *not* the procedure our Lord is suggesting for the Christian who wants God's answer day by day. For this individual only a day by day study of God's Word will suffice.

Frequently Christians scoff at the idea of finding God's will about their specific situations revealed in God's Word. They suggest that the Bible contains only general or guiding principles useful in developing a Christian life-style. How sad that they have reduced the living word to dead formulas.

There are those who question the idea of finding a word from God about specific situations on the basis that it is too subjective. When asked what method they propose, they generally indicate a procedure that involves a little gathering of information, a little prayer, and then playing their "hunch." Nothing could be more subjective.

Even looking for open doors presents problems as a satisfying method of consistently operating within the will of God. I have discovered that often, just before I learn what God wants for me, the devil will make it possible for me to receive what I want for myself, and I confuse the two. The door is always open to the paths of destruction.

Please do not misunderstand. Gathering information about an issue is useful; having a settled peace in your heart is important; and open doors can indeed be an indication that God is in a certain matter. But *consistent study of God's Word along a prescribed pattern (whatever plan of Bible study you may have) is the key.* Remember that no plan is going to make you want to read the Bible. *The secret of conquering any resistance to Bible reading is to read the Bible for the purpose of meeting the Lord and discovering his will.*

How will you know when you have found God's revealed will regarding the specific need about which you are praying? The best answer is that you will just know intuitively as the Holy

Spirit speaks to you. Do you remember Colossians 2:6? "As you have therefore received Christ Jesus the Lord, so walk ye in him." This means that in the same fashion the Holy Spirit bears witness that you are a Christian (1 John 4:13) he will bear witness that a specific passage is his prescription for your problem.

One day I was asked about this issue of *knowing* something is a revelation of God's will. God gave me a phrase that I have used often since that time. "A Bible promise is not a verse you grab. It is a verse that grabs you as you in the context of your need apply a surrendered life to a consistent study of the Scripture."

Step 5: I Make a Faith Request

If you have determined that God's Word is true, regardless of what the world says; and God has given you his Word regarding your specific situation, then you simply agree with him. You are actually making a "faith request" according to the Bible promise he has given you. When you do this you have entered into an aggressive cooperation with God's revealed will. First John 5:14 says that prayer confidence comes from asking according to his will.

Suppose you decided to give your child a bicycle for Christmas. Perhaps, in fact, you had already purchased it and now it is stored in the attic. You must encourage your child to want what you want to give him.

"Son," you ask, "What would you like for Christmas?" "Electric trains," he might reply. Since this is not a suitable answer, you begin to point out the merits of bicycle ownership and the joy that comes from riding a bike.

As Christmas nears, you begin to be concerned. Your son has not yet agreed with your plans for his gift. Finally he says, "You know, I've been doing a lot of thinking about what you've said. I believe you are right. I sure would like a bicycle." What does he get? Exactly what he asked for. This illustration helps us begin to understand what praying in faith is all about. We find God's will and then pray in accord with it. This is joyful news to the person who understands that God always wants what is best for us.

In the Scripture we are told both to "pray without ceasing" (1 Thess. 5:17), and to pray specific, onetime prayers of commitment (Ps. 37:5). Some imagine a conflict here, but again we find the answer by returning to Colossians 2:6 for our pattern in prayer. The prayer without ceasing is the prayer you pray *until* you find the revealed will of God. Abraham's intercession for Lot (Gen. 18:23-33), which will be discussed in a later chapter, is a good example. Once you find the revealed will of God you simply commit it to God and act according to his prescribed course. If you pray again about the matter it is simply to express gratitude that he is working in the situation regardless of how things "appear" to be working out.

Once you have made your faith request, agreeing to enter into aggressive cooperation with God's will, you are ready to experience the final, exciting step toward praying with success.

Step 6: God Hears and Grants

"And this is the confidence that we have in him, that, if we ask any thing according to his will, he heareth us: And if we know that he hears us, whatsoever we ask, we know that we have the petitions that we desired of him" (1 John 5:14-15).

It is often said that the person with the argument is at the mercy of the person with the experience. Perhaps the following experience will illustrate both the basic principles involved in praying with success and the remarkable manner in which God often hears and grants.

On one occasion I found myself swept up in a great moving of God's Spirit because of a promise God had made to a young woman who was praying for her father. Several men were gathered for a prayer meeting in our church when I heard the office phone begin to ring. There was such a persistence about the ringing that I finally slipped out of the prayer meeting, made my way to the office, and lifted the receiver. I was surprised to hear, on the other end, the voice of a college friend I had not seen for several years.

My friend explained that she was working at a "half-way house" on the California coast. Then she explained the reason for her call. She had met and ministered to a young woman who had since returned to her home in a Western state. As a new Christian, the young woman had become burdened for her friends and family, especially for her father. God had given her a scriptural assurance that he would bring revival to her home town and she was acting on his promise. She had secured the use of the high school gymnasium for a three-day period. Then, at a loss for what to do next, she had called my friend for advice. They agreed to ask a preacher to come and hold services.

"Will you come?" asked my friend. I assured to her that I was sympathetic with what was happening. But since there seemed to be a lack of local church sponsorship, and since the revival was scheduled only two weeks away, I would be unable to come. "Pray about it," she insisted, "and call me later." I agreed, but I already knew I would say no again.

I returned to the prayer meeting and related the incident to the men. They responded in a remarkable fashion, especially considering the negative attitude of their pastor. "I think you should go and I'll pay for the ticket," said one. "I'll go with you!" exclaimed another. Two weeks later four of us drove into the town late at night. We were met by the young woman. She and a friend led us to the house where we would be staying.

When the door was opened, we found ourselves in the middle of a prayer meeting. Brokenhearted, but confident of the power of God, people were claiming their friends for Christ, one at a time. We began to pray with them and the prayer meeting continued until the early morning hours.

Even though we sensed that God was working, we were amazed the next evening to find the gymnasium filled with young people and adults. God's power fell on the meeting and swept through the town. During those three days, people from every corner of life, almost two hundred of them, confessed Christ as Savior and Lord. Churches were filled the following Sunday; and Bible study groups were formed which continued for a great while afterward. It all began when God found an earnest young woman, crying out to him at a time of need, who was willing to act on his revealed will.

When you decide to enter into the abiding life, and consistently seek his will through his word, you will discover that God is eager to make a covenant with you. God always keeps his promises.

5
Characteristics of the Intercessor

Picture a thief moving stealthily through a home. The father awakens and quietly moves in the direction of the children's room where he hears the burglar's footsteps. As the father switches on the light, he catches the thief in the act of placing a small radio in a sack. The terrified thief grabs the arm of one of the children and jerks the child close to him as an act of defense. The thief moves toward the door, sack in one hand and panic-stricken child in the other. What will the father do? Using the prayer life of the average Christian as his example, the father will try to rescue the sack.

It is an unfortunate testimony to our sad spiritual state, that, for the most part, we miss the major purpose of prayer. God has given us prayer not primarily as a method for getting "things" or changing circumstances but as our means of jointly cooperating with him in his great plan for the redemption of the lost.

A clear example of intercession is recorded in the eighteenth chapter of Genesis. The Lord and two other messengers met with Abraham and Sarah to tell them about the promise of a son, through whom all the nations of the world would be blessed. Afterwards, as they set their faces toward Sodom, "Abraham went with them to bring them on the way" (v. 16). The Lord responded by asking, "Shall I hide from Abraham that thing which I do? . . . For I know him, that he will command his children and his household after him, and they shall keep the way of the Lord, to do justice and judgment" (vv. 17-19). The Lord then explained his purpose for going to Sodom and Gomorrah by noting that

39

their "sin is very grievous" (v. 20). Abraham became distressed because his nephew, Lot, lived in Sodom. The Scripture records that "the men turned their faces from thence, and went toward Sodom: but Abraham stood yet before the Lord" (v. 22). It is here that Abraham begins to intercede for the welfare of Lot and his family. Persistent in prayer, he finally secured this promise from the Lord: "I will not destroy it [Sodom] for ten's sake" (v. 32). It is then that the "Lord went his way . . . and Abraham returned unto his place" (v. 33).

From these verses we see that intercession requires a "falling in," or as previously stated an "aggressive cooperation with God," along the lines of his revealed will. Additionally, we see that intercession involves an activity before God on behalf of a specific person or persons. In this chapter we will examine the qualities necessary in the life of a Christian who desires to enter into the ministry of intercession. In the next chapter we will examine the activity of intercession.

The Ignored Symbolism of the Tabernacle

It is unfortunate that many Christians consider those passages of Scriptures about the tabernacle in the wilderness a drudgery to read. It is inconceivable that God would admit such passages to the Scripture if they were not designed to reveal certain significant truths. I believe the design of the tabernacle reveals the ministries which Christ performs in the life of every believer. Refer to the diagram as you read the following interpretation.

The tabernacle can be seen to represent the three basic areas of our lives. The outer courtyard surrounded by a high curtain represents the body, or externally visible part of our being. The holy place, a place of daily activity within the confines of the tentlike structure, represents the soul. The holy of holies represents the Spirit, or place of communion with the Lord.

Each component within the tabernacle area symbolizes a specific aspect of the ministry of Christ. For instance, entrance was gained

OUTER COURTYARD

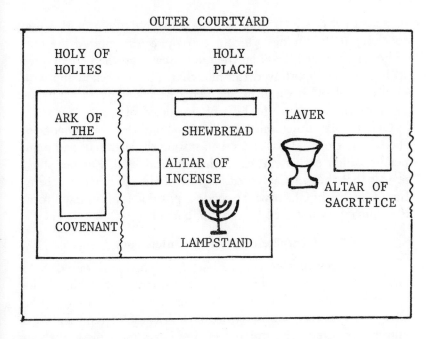

by way of (1) the altar of sacrifice and (2) the laver of cleansing. This can serve as a constant reminder that we should (1) lay down our lives for the One who laid down his life for us; and (2) there could be no fellowship with God apart from the cleansing of sin. In the holy place we find (1) the table of shewbread, (2) the golden lampstand, and (3) the altar of incense. These items remind us that Christ is the "bread of life" (John 6:35), the "true light, which lights every man that comes into the world," and he "ever liveth to make intercession" (Heb. 7:25).

The ark of the covenant was placed in the holy of holies. The ark contained the tablets of the law, a pot of manna, and, on occasion, Aaron's rod that budded. These items can be seen to represent (1) the principles of God which reveal sin, (2) his unfailing provision, and (3) the resurrection life of Christ, unfailing provision for men cursed by the law. On top of the ark was the mercy seat over which were fashioned two cherubims with wings touching at the middle. Once a year the priest entered the holy of holies, sprinkled blood on the mercy seat, and then communed with God. This portrayed the fact that ultimate fellowship with God is available because in his mercy he is willing to apply the blood of the Lamb to the lives of sin-cursed men.

One further thing must be noted about the components of the tabernacle. God was specific in stating the materials and manner by which each item was fashioned and used. Further study reveals that their characteristics represent the specific characteristics in the life of Christ which made it possible for him to perform the ministry symbolized by the component.

Characteristics of the Intercessor

The purpose of this chapter, as mentioned previously, is to examine the qualities which must be present in the life of the Christian who desires to enter the ministry of intercession. The altar of incense serves as our pattern because it represents his ministry of intercession for us and the qualities in his life which make such a ministry possible. These qualities are specifically outlined in Exodus 30:1-10. I want to mention three qualities which appear to be of particular significance.

Position

Intercession is as much the taking of a position as it is the making of a petition. Genesis 30:6 states that the altar of incense is to be placed "before the veil that is by the ark of the testimony, before the mercy seat that is over the testimony, where I will meet with thee." In other words, the altar of incense was positioned before the mercy seat, between it and everything else in the tabernacle. It was the last component which the high priest saw before entering the holy of holies. Taken literally an intercessor's position is before God, and between God and the person for whom he is interceding.

Here again it is worthy to note Abraham's intercession for Lot recorded in Genesis 18. "Abraham stood yet before the Lord" (v. 22). Abraham was before the Lord and between the Lord and Sodom where Lot was living in sin.

To position yourself before someone is to say, "There is a matter which you and I must settle before I can continue on." That is what Abraham was saying. That is what you will say if you engage in intercession. Notice a certain boldness here: "Lord I have such a burden I do not feel I can continue on until it is settled." While a Christian should be concerned for all people, it is apparent that on certain occasions, God gives us a burden for a specific individual or individuals. At that time we *must* settle the issue with God. And so we assume the position of an intercessor.

Perseverance

In Genesis 30:7-8 God gives instruction regarding the use of the altar of incense. Incense was to be burned both morning and evening, and it was to be "a perpetual incense before the Lord throughout your generations" (v. 8). Here is where great spiritual battles are often won or lost. At issue is the willingness to "pray without ceasing" *until* God reveals his will about the issue of concern.

Persevering prayer is an experience about which few Christians can testify. They are willing, when asked, to pray for certain individuals. Perhaps they even enter that person's name on a daily prayer list for frequent consideration. But, for most, little is known about being bowed before God in spirit (if not in body) until God reveals his will.

Individuals engaged in the ministry of intercession have a hard time thinking of anything else. While they may have before them the daily demands of their occupations, even these are carried out with the inner man bowed before God.

Listen to Abraham as he intercedes for Lot. Here is a man who prays with urgency and determination.

And Abraham drew near, and said, Wilt thou also destroy the righteous with the wicked? Peradventure there be fifty righteous within the city: wilt thou also destroy and not spare the place for the fifty righteous that are therein? That be far from thee to do after this manner, to slay the righteous with the wicked: and that the righteous should be as the wicked, that be far from thee: Shall not the Judge of all the earth do right?

And the Lord said, If I find in Sodom fifty righteous within the city, then I will spare all the place for their sakes. And Abraham answered and said, Behold now, I have taken upon me to speak unto the Lord, which am but dust and ashes: Peradventure there shall lack five of the fifty righteous: wilt thou destroy all the city for lack of five? And he said, If I find there forty and five, I will not destroy it.

And he spake unto him yet again, and said, Peradventure there shall be forty found there. And he said, I will not do it for forty's sake. And he said unto him, Oh let not the Lord be angry, and I will speak: Peradventure there shall thirty be found there. And he said, I will not do it, if I find thirty there. And he said, Behold now, I have taken upon me to speak unto the Lord: Peradventure there shall be twenty found there. And he said, I will not destroy it for twenty's sake. And he said, Oh let not the Lord be angry, and I will speak yet but this once: Peradventure ten shall be found there. And he said, I will not destroy it for ten's sake. And the Lord went his way, as soon as he had left communing with Abraham: and Abraham returned unto his place (Gen. 18:23-33).

Note that Abraham's persistant appeal is to the Lord's righteousness. He is not trying to impress the Lord with his or Lot's credentials. Lot's salvation will be based on a sovereign act of God in response to Abraham's prayer.

Frequently Christians ask me to pray with them about people for whom they have definite concern. In the following days these Christians make no mention of their concern. It is apparent that there is no great burden on their heart. Occasionally someone who makes such a prayer request appears to have assumed the position of intercessor. Every time I see them they report on the status of the individual for whom they have asked prayer. "Please continue to pray," they will insist tearfully as our conversation ends. Often it is with tears of joy that they report "victory" as God brings blessing to their lives by allowing them to enter into aggressive cooperation in his great work.

Luke 11:5-8 records Jesus' parable emphasizing the importance of shameless persistence in prayer. "And he said unto them, Which of you shall have a friend, and shall go unto him at midnight, and say unto him, Friend, lend me three loaves: For a friend of mine in his journey is come to me, and I have nothing to set before him? And he from within shall answer and say, Trouble me not: the door is now shut, and my children are with me in bed; I cannot rise and give thee. I say unto you, Though he will not rise and give him, because he is his friend, yet because of his importunity he will rise and give him as many as he needeth."

It was not the size of the need, the cause of the need, or the credentials of the one in need which finally secured the answer. It was his "importunity" or shameless persistence. The Lord concluded the parable with this statement: "Ask [literally: and keep on asking], and it shall be given you; seek [and keep on seeking], and ye shall find; knock [and keep on knocking], and it shall be opened unto you" (v. 9). It is little wonder that the enemy seeks so actively to destroy the Christian's determination to persevere in prayer.

Purity

There was a strict formula for the type of incense to be burned on the altar in the tabernacle. God admonished the priests, "You shall offer no strange incense thereon, nor burnt sacrifice, nor meat offering; neither shall you pour drink offering thereon" (Ex. 30:9). Only pure incense, according to the formula, was to be offered.

If there is one point more than any other, where the Christian is defeated in prayer, it is at the point of personal purity. God hates sin. It is an abomination to him. It cost him his son. We fail to deal with sin in biblical terms. Instead we call it a "bad habit," "personality trait," "shortcoming," or "character flaw." Some people feel that sin can be isolated in an otherwise righteous life. That is ridiculous. It is like telling your friends you are in perfect health and only your leg has cancer. Sin in part affects the whole. Your sin, no matter how secret, affects your ability and the ability of your church to pray.

Christians seem especially susceptible to sins of presumption (see Ps. 19:13); sins which presume on God's love and forgiveness. Here is a man, seated in a worship service, just dying to get out so he can indulge in his favorite habit. His is a planned sin which says in essence, "God, you are loving and forgiving. Turn your head while I sin. But be quick to forgive when I ask."

Our prayers are answered because we pray "in Jesus' name," that is, on the basis of what he has accomplished and who he is. How many times have you kneeled to pray, only to be confronted by the master of accusation, Satan himself. "You don't really think this is going to do any good, do you? It never has before. Your life is no example of victory. How can you presume to be in touch with God?" Defeated by those words, or similar, you throw in the towel, failing to claim the great power of God as effective in your life or that of another. Satan used your sin as his tool of defeat.

It is worth remembering that intercession involves "falling in" with God in aggressive cooperation with his revealed will. God can have no fellowship with sin. The psalmist writes: "Who shall ascend into the hill of the Lord? or who shall stand in his holy place? He that hath clean hands and a pure heart" (Ps. 24:3-4). God speaks to his people through Isaiah: "Behold, the Lord's hand is not shortened, that it cannot save; neither his ear heavy, that it cannot hear. But your iniquities have separated between you and your God, and your sins have hidden his face from you, that he will not hear" (Isa. 59:1-2). The heart's cry of every Christian who would labor in the fields of intercession should be, "Create in me a clean heart, O God; and renew a right spirit within me" (Ps. 51:10).

The person who would participate in Olympic competition spends years preparing his body and mind for a specific event of only temporal importance. In light of the billions of people who are away from God, how can we afford to spend less effort and time preparing our hearts and lives for the eternally significant work of intercession?

6
The Biblical Method
of Intercession

There is a difference between praying for people and genuine intercession. The apostle Paul referred to this distinction when he wrote: "I exhort, therefore, that first of all, supplications, prayers, intercessions, and giving of thanks, be made for all men" (1 Tim. 2:1). Here prayer and intercession are considered as separate activities. While intercession involves prayer, not all praying for others is intercessory in nature.

Perhaps the following illustration will help you see the difference between praying for people and genuine intercession. As a pastor I receive many calls requesting that I pray for people. In each case I seek to respond as conscientiously as possible. I often pray with the caller before our conversation ends. It is a blessed privilege, especially when I hear later of answered prayer. On some occasions, however, God will lay on my heart the burden of intercession.

Such was the case several years ago when I received an urgent call from a distressed new father. What should have been an expression of joy was instead a plea for help. "Pray for my son!" he said. "The doctors have discovered a serious difficulty and say there is a good possibility he might die in the next few hours." I assured him of my prayers and told him I would meet him at the hospital in a matter of minutes.

As I was preparing to leave, God suddenly brought to my heart the necessity of interceding for that newborn baby. I slipped to my knees beside my bed and began to pray. At the same time I searched the Scripture passage I had been reading when the young father called. Suddenly God spoke to my heart through his word, giving the assurance that the child would not only survive this crisis, but live to become a great witness for God. Thanking God for his word I drove to the hospital where the exuberant parents met me. They had just received word from their doctors that the child had suddenly responded to treatment and would most surely be well enough to go home in a few days.

Why had God given the burden of intercession at this time and not some other? I don't know. I do know that it is always thrilling to discover he has chosen us to play an integral part in the lives of others through the practice of prayer. Why did God choose to give a revelation of his will in a matter of minutes, when on other occasions it does not come for months, or even years. I don't know. The testimony of the Scripture is that before God performs a great ministry he generally reveals the nature of that ministry to someone who is praying.

In James 4:17 we are reminded that "to him that knoweth to do good and doeth it not, to him it is sin." Since we established the fact that to pray is not an option open to the Christian, but rather the fulfillment of God's command, it is evident that not praying is a sin. There are many Christians who feel God's leadership to enter the ministry of intercession. They are not certain, however, just what methods to follow. In this chapter we will study the biblical method of intercession.

A pattern for intercession is found in chapters 32 and 33 of Exodus. Moses is returning from Mount Sinai. Assuming Moses had left them for good, the Israelites had encouraged Aaron to make a golden calf. When Moses arrived at the camp, they were worshiping with drunken revelry and idolatry.

After breaking the tablets of the law at the base of Mount Sinai, Moses turned his attention to the sin of Israel. First he ground the calf into powder, poured it into the water, and made the Israelites drink it. (An excellent example of the way God can turn an object of delight into the object of discipline.) Then

Moses gathered to him the sons of Levi, men who openly professed to be on the Lord's side. They began to slay with the sword the ungodly Israelites, killing three thousand people that day. There was no question but that God's wrath was being poured out that day.

The next day Moses returned to Mount Sinai to intercede for the people. Notice the following pattern of intercession:

Establishing the Right Purpose

"You have sinned a great sin," Moses said to the children of Israel, "And now I will go up unto the Lord; perhaps I can make atonement for your sin" (Ex. 32:30, RSV). Moses assumed the position of an intercessor ("I will go up unto the Lord") for a specific purpose expressed by the word "atonement." In its original form the word atonement meant simply to "cover." In the biblical sense it refers to an act of grace by which offenses were "covered" so that fellowship could be restored between the offender and the one offended. In other words, Moses determined to plead with God to cover the sins of Israel so that fellowship between God and the Israelites could be maintained. Such an act would be based entirely upon God's grace or willingness to grant an unmerited favor.

The proper purpose of intercession is seeking to secure the grace of God for an individual, or individuals, so that fellowship with God and usefulness for God will be established or maintained. The major issue of intercession is God's will. Frequently someone says, "I am praying for a certain person to receive physical healing," or "I am praying for someone who desperately needs a job." Such prayers certainly express the desires of our hearts. And, of course, we cannot "fool" God into thinking that, in our hearts, we desire less for the individual. What does God want for that individual? What does he see as necessary to bring an individual into fellowship with himself? More importantly, are you willing to wait before him and pray in agreement to his revealed will?

I have heard sincere Christians say to a person undergoing some trial, "I have prayed that God would work this out in a certain way, and I just know he's going to do it." Too often they do not "know" but only "hope." They may be trying to "nail God down" by staking his reputation on their verbal confession. The result is only added delay in bringing the individual into conformity with God's will.

Consider the loving mother who prays, "Lord, bring my son home and don't let him get hurt." It may be God's will for him to return home. It may also be true that, apart from the "hurt" he may experience, he will return the same as when he left and none the better. This is not to say that we should throw up our hands in resignation to sickness, heartache, or other tragic situations. On the contrary! The basic purpose of intercession should be to establish or maintain a fellowship with God that will only occur as a result of his grace.

Notice that Moses made no promises, raised no false hopes, nor gave unfounded assurances. "You have sinned a great sin . . . perhaps I can make atonement for your sin." He realized that apart from an act of God's grace the children of Israel could no longer enjoy the presence of God.

Addressing the Problem

"And Moses returned unto the Lord and said, Oh, this people have sinned a great sin, and have made them gods of gold" (Ex. 32:31). Moses admitted both the sinfulness of Israel and the specific manner in which the sin was manifested.

It is strange that often we do not speak to the One who reads our hearts about what is really in our hearts. We attempt to impress God with the credentials of the person for whom we are praying. Consider a mother praying for a wayward son. Between sobs she cries out, "Lord, you know my son is a good boy!" If that is the case, why is she beseeching God for an act of mercy? The truth could be that her son is wicked and deserves far worse!

True intercession does not seek to ignore the facts. Moses did not say, "Now Lord, you know these folks have had to put up with a lot of trouble. You know they are good at heart, You know that, given a second chance, they will do better." He said instead, "These people have sinned a great sin!"

What about the Christian who is living in fellowship with God but undergoing some great trial? Perhaps God is calling you to enter into the position of an intercessor for that individual and to you there is no apparent sin. For instance, a fine Christian is experiencing a grave physical illness, and God is leading you to intercede. How should you pray? Admit the problem, as specific as possible, and remember that you are requesting an act of grace that will enable the individual to maintain a close and useful fellowship with God.

On the eve of his crucifixion Jesus was moved to intercede not only for his disciples "but for them also which shall believe on me through their [the disciples'] word; That they all may be one, as thou Father, art in me, and I in thee that they also may be one in us; that the world may believe that thou hast sent me" (John 17:20-21). Notice the two basic issues of this intercession: (1) Fellowship with the Lord, "that they may be one in us," and; (2) Usefulness, "that the world may believe."

Intercession is more than praying in general terms for a person. It is not an attempt to play on God's sympathy. Intercession is seeking the mind of God. Therefore, it is important to specify the issue at stake. Do not overlook the importance of addressing the problem in specific terms.

Presenting the Plea

"Yet now, if thou wilt forgive their sin—; and if not, blot me, I pray thee out of thy book which thou hast written" (Ex. 32:32). Having addressed the problem Moses made a specific plea, "forgive their sin." Notice several things about the manner in which Moses presented his plea:

1. He was still seeking the mind of God. "If thou wilt." As of that moment he had not secured a revelation of God's will

regarding the future of Israel. Faith is based upon fact. It springs from the truth as revealed through God's word. Moses awaited God's final judgment of the situation.

2. He asked God to deal with the problem, not the symptom. "Forgive their sin." The problem is sin, manifested here by making a god of gold. True intercession must deal with the root causes, rather than symptoms. A man with tuberculosis may have a serious cough. You may pray that his cough would cease, but you may not be dealing with the real problem. Again it is important to know the specific issue at stake.

3. He was, by identification, positioning himself between God and the people for whom he was interceding. "And if not, blot me, I pray thee, out of thy book which thou hast written." It is of interest that Moses knew about the "Lamb's book of life" (Rev. 21:27). Of greater interest is the fact that Moses was dead serious about his intercession. So much so, that he staked his life on the outcome. Intercession was not just one of the things Moses was doing. It was *the* thing which occupied him until God gave an answer.

Jesus is the great example of positioning oneself, by identification, between God and the individual for whom you are praying. He "made himself of no reputation, and took upon him the form of a servant, and was made in the likeness of men; And being found in fashion as a man, he humbled himself and became obedient unto death, even the death of the cross" (Phil. 2:7-8).

An intercessor literally feels with the person for whom he is praying. An intercessor is willing to go to any length to secure an act of God's grace for the individual. This is why so few Christians enter into the labor of intercession. It is a most demanding type of ministry!

Securing a Promise

Apparently the intercession of Moses for the children of Israel lasted over a period of many days. God agreed to allow Moses to lead the Israelites to Canaan, promising protection and direction, but, he said, "I will not go up in the midst of thee" (Ex. 33:3). Moses realized that the unique distinction of Israel was the presence of God and so he continued to intercede. A tabernacle for intercession was built outside the camp for "every one which sought the Lord" (Ex. 33:7). There Moses and the Lord talked "face to face as a man speaketh unto his friend" (Ex. 33:11).

It was during this time that Moses called to mind what God has already promised concerning the welfare of Israel (Ex. 33:12) and pled for the presence of God to be restored. "For wherein shall it be known here that I and your people have found grace in your sight? is it not in that thou goest with us? so shall we be separated, I and thy people, from all the people that are upon the face of the earth" (Ex. 33:16). Moses requested an act of grace that would allow fellowship with God and usefulness for God.

Finally the Lord said to Moses, "I will do this thing also that thou hast spoken; for thou hast found grace in my sight, and I know thee by name" (Ex. 33:17). Just as Abraham had interceded for backslidden Lot, so Moses had interceded for Israel and secured the promise of God.

During a prayer time several years ago I listened as a grief-stricken father shared the burdens of his heart. His daughter had left home after a continuing series of family conflicts. Several days of searching had failed to locate her. Her parents had discovered further evidence that her rebellious attitude had brought her into the company of the most questionable type of individuals.

Fortunately for both the girl and her family, her parents knew how to employ the biblical method of intercession. After weeks of prayer and searching in the Word, the father related that God had given him a Bible promise regarding the welfare of his daughter and indeed his entire family. "Thy wife shall be as a fruitful vine by the sides of thine house; thy children like olive plants round about thy table. Behold, that thus shall the man be blessed who feareth the Lord" (Ps. 128:3-4).

As is so often the case, the situation seemed to worsen almost immediately. There was virtually no communication with the daughter. The pressures associated with her absence created additional problems for the family. Still these faithful parents prayed according to God's revealed will.

After almost a year I received a telephone call from the daughter requesting a conference. Although she had wanted to avoid meeting her parents, the Lord ordained a providential reunion in the church parking lot before she entered the building. Imagine my surprise to find all three of them waiting at my office door.

During the moments that followed I heard a firsthand testimony to the effectiveness of intercession. The young lady related that, months earlier, she had married, only to have her husband arrested shortly afterward on a drug charge. While in jail he had been introduced to Christ and was born into the family of God. Calling his young wife to the jail he related his experience with Christ, led her to make a similar commitment, and encouraged her to locate her parents so that they both might ask forgiveness. She had requested the conference to ask how best to go about reestablishing a relationship with her parents. By the time of the conference it was all settled.

Over the next few months the parents visited their son-in-law on a regular basis, assured him of their support and encouraged him in Christian growth. Since then he has been released from prison. Both he and his wife are actively serving the Lord. Both parents have had the thrill of seeing their entire family assembled "like olive plants round about thy table."

God is eager to make a covenant with those who will enter into the ministry of intercession. Like these parents you can join the ranks with the likes of Abraham and Moses who successfully interceded by securing the promise of God.

7
The Danger of Not Getting a Word from God

Men respond in various ways to the gospel message. Some are cut to the heart and cry, "What must I do to be saved?" Others see the sense of it, feel the need of salvation, but stubbornly refuse the grace of God. Still others consider it all a foolish exercise of man's overactive imagination.

It is interesting to note that Christians, likewise, respond in various ways to an encouragement to "walk by faith, not by sight." For some there is an immediate acceptance and ready application. Others who see the sense and feel the need are reluctant to step out on God's Word alone. Still others scoff at the idea that God has a word pertinent to their specific need. These people see the Bible as a collection of nothing more than general principles. They stumble on, choosing to believe what the world says, rather than what God's Word says about their specific situation.

Admittedly, just as there is no way to argue a man into salvation, there is no way to argue a Christian into operating on the basis of God's will as revealed through his Word. It is worth noting, however, the dangers that await those who fail to get a word from God. That is the purpose of the following study taken from the ninth and tenth chapters of Joshua.

After the death of Moses, Joshua was given the responsibility of leading the Israelites into Canaan and subduing the land. God had strictly commanded that no alliances were to be made with the inhabitants of Canaan. After the fall of Jericho and Ai, various kings in Canaan determined to band their armies together in an attempt to defeat the Israelites. The men of Gibeon refused to join the Canaanite alliance. They saw that the power of God was with the Israelites. Knowing the Israelites' stubborn refusal to make treaties with any tribe in Canaan, the men of Gibeon devised a subtle plot to draw the Israelites into an alliance. They pretended to be citizens of a country outside Canaan.

Ambassadors, dressed in old garments and carrying spoiled food, were sent to the camp of Israel. On the back of their animals were old sacks and torn wineskins. Arriving in the Israelite camp at Gilgal, they said, "We have come from a far country; now therefore make ye a league with us" (Josh. 9:6).

The men of Israel were suspicious at first and took them to Joshua who asked, "Who are you? And where do you come from?" (Josh. 9:8, RSV). The Gibeons insisted that they had come from a distant country, not Canaan, because of all they had heard about the power of God resting on the Israelites. Under further questioning, they asked the men of Israel to notice their clothing, food, old sacks, and wineskins. They insisted that all these items were new and fresh when they had departed from their country.

Joshua and his captains were convinced by what they saw and heard. They "took of their victuals, and asked not counsel at the mouth of the Lord. And Joshua made peace with them, and made a league with them, to let them live; and the princes of the congregation sware unto them" (Josh. 9:14-15). This was one of the most costly mistakes in the history of Israel. All because they "asked not counsel at the mouth of the Lord."

Easily Fooled by the Words of Men

"From a very far country thy servants are come," said the Gibeonites to Joshua, "because of the name of the Lord thy God; for we have heard of the fame of him, and all that he did in Egypt, And all that he did to the two kings of the Amorites, that were beyond Jordan, to Sihon king of Heshbon, and to Og king of Bashan, which was at Ashtaroth. Wherefore our elders and all the inhabitants of our country spake to us, saying, Take

victuals with you for the journey, and go to meet them, and say
unto them, We are your servants: therefore, now, make ye a league
with us" (Josh. 9:9-11).

Pretended spirituality, flattery, humility is all present in this
well-rehearsed plea presented to Joshua. Many unsuspecting Christians have been talked into unholy alliances because the word
of man was their highest counsel. Think how often you have
heard someone say, "He made it *sound* so good" or "It wasn't
at all like they *said* it would be." The Christian who fails to
seek God's revealed will through his Word limits his counsel to
other men, and his opinion of their opinions. As such, he is easily
misled and frequently falls prey to the "father of lies" (John 8:44,
RSV).

Several years ago God reminded my wife and me that he was
interested in every aspect of our lives—even the purchase of a
new automobile. Our family was growing and we were in need
of more substantial transportation. After visiting the showrooms
of several dealers, we finally decided on the purchase of a very
basic model station wagon. Before we made the purchase I visited
a Christian brother, who was a member of my church. He told
me that he was acquainted with a man in the automobile business
and he was sure I could get a "good deal" from him.

We visited the man in a neighboring town. True to our expecta-
tions, he showed us a luxury model station wagon and quoted a
price several hundred dollars below the cost of the one we intended
to buy. I just knew it must be God's will. The deal came on
the basis of advice of a fine Christian man; it was more automobile
than we ever dreamed of owning; and it cost much less. (I assumed
God was trying to save every penny he could!)

With my wife's encouragement, I agreed to seek a Bible promise
before acting. After several days of prayer and searching, we were
impressed with Proverbs 4:14-15. "Enter not into the path of
the wicked, and go not in the way of evil men. Avoid it, pass
not by it, turn from it, and pass away." "Surely," I thought,

"God must be referring to the car we originally intended to purchase." But, in my heart, I clearly knew the Lord was referring to the "good deal."

I called the dealer and explained that it was not God's will for us to purchase the automobile. He responded with a few choice words about preachers! We proceeded, with settled hearts, according to the original plan. But I was a little confused and a lot disappointed. Several weeks later it became clear that God had rescued us! The newspaper carried a story about the man with the "good deal." He was accused of taking old, high-mileage automobiles, fixing them up like new, and selling them to unsuspecting customers. Since then I have often thought of the words of the psalmist who said of the Word of God, "Moreover by them is thy servant warned" (Ps. 19:11).

Easily Fooled by Visible Evidence

"Look at the evidence," insisted the Gibeonites. "This our bread we took hot for our provision out of our houses on the day we came forth to go unto you; but now, behold, it is dry and mouldy; And these bottles of wine, which we filled, were new, and behold, they be rent; and there our garments and our shoes are become old by reason of the very long journey" (Josh. 9:12-13). The visible evidence was carefully contrived as the key of their subtle plot.

Most of us would confess to struggling long over a difficult decision only to make the final choice on the basis of flimsy, but tangible evidence. For most people, including many Christians, seeing is believing. Since "the children of this world are in their generation wiser than the children of light" (Luke 16:8), their primary method of operation involves an assault on the physical senses. Christians who neglect getting a word from God when making decisions are easy prey and often fall as victims to worldly or satanic devices. Eve, for instance, was tempted to sin primarily on this basis. She "saw that the tree was good for food, and that it was pleasant to the eyes" (Gen. 3:6). David's great sin was first conceived on the basis of visual evidence alone (2 Sam. 11:2).

Had Joshua reflected for a moment he would have recalled that for forty years he and the children of Israel had wandered in the wilderness because they neglected the Word of God and acted on the basis of a visual impression. God had said, "search the land of Canaan which I give unto the children of Israel" (Num. 13:2). Having made the search, ten of the spies reported that, "the people are strong that dwell in the land, and the cities are walled, and very great; . . . and we were in our own sight as grasshoppers, and so we were in their sight" (Num. 13:28,33). Based on this report, the children of Israel rebelled against God, choosing to walk by sight rather than by faith.

How often must we be reminded that to neglect the word of God results in being easily fooled by what we see. Joshua should have recalled the great loss at Ai only a short while earlier. God had allowed them to suffer defeat because one man "saw among the spoils a goodly Babylonish garment, and two hundred shekels of silver, and a wedge of gold of fifty shekels weight and . . . coveted them, and took them" (Josh. 7:21). It is difficult to live victoriously when much of what we do and own result from being easily fooled by what we have seen.

Indifferent to Inner Reservations
Which May Be the Voice of God

"Peradventure you dwell among us," said the men of Israel; "and how shall we make a league with you?" (Josh. 9:7). Their conversation reveals some inner reservations as to the trustworthiness of the Gibeonites. That inner reservation was actually the result of their sensitivity to God. God was encouraging them to seek counsel. The counsel of God was ignored and a treacherous agreement was established.

God often makes us sensitive to the fact that we are entering into a situation where his counsel would be profitable. If, however, we are determined to make the decision on our own, we will ignore those divinely initiated inner reservations.

I remember sharing on this particular subject during a worship service. Afterwards I encountered a man who confessed that, on several occasions, he had actually rushed a decision-making process because he was afraid that, given more time, he might choose not to make the purchase. In virtually every case the decisions had brought him great distress. Isn't this the reason the world often says, "If you buy now, you will get such a better deal than if you wait to buy later"?

Satan often uses the pressure of time. But God is the creator of time. After all, don't we measure time by the things God has created (revolution of the earth on its axis, etc.)? This means that time is on the side of the person who is on the side of God. The Christian who will wait for the word of God can be assured that God will always provide a way of doing what he commands us to do. In fact, we will see how God later made time stand still so that Joshua could gain victory in a battle which resulted from his alliance with the Gibeonites.

On frequent occasions I hear from those who are experiencing problems in marriage. "I must confess," they often say, "I had some reservations prior to the marriage." Some even go so far as to admit they were firmly convinced the relationship would not be ideal. But since the invitations were sent and cancellation would be embarrassing, they forged ahead, ignoring their inner reservations which were, in actuality the voice of God. Certainly God has a word regarding the kind of behavior that will bring peace to their present marriage. But how many broken homes could be averted if the couple would wait for a clear understanding of God's will prior to marriage.

Similar situations often develop in church-staff relationships. Often individuals, who firmly declare they are brought together under the leadership of the Lord, respond differently when trouble is brewing. They confess to having experienced inner reservations from the beginning. But everything looked and sounded so right! Surely God would give peace of heart and mind once they began serving together. But it never came! How different things might have been had both parties waited upon the Lord to give divine guidance through his word.

When the Lord gives us the discernment that further light is needed, it is imperative to follow the advice of Proverbs 3:5-6: "Trust in the Lord with all thine heart; and lean not unto thine own understanding. In all thy ways acknowledge him, and he shall direct thy paths." In prayer we are seeking the mind of God. A reluctance to discover his will indicates either an exaggerated self-confidence or the fear that God will not give an endorsement to our selfish desires.

A Commitment to the World

If we persist in our refusal to seek counsel from God, we will ultimately make a costly commitment to the world. "And the men took of their victuals, and asked not counsel at the mouth of the Lord. And Joshua made peace with them, and made a league, with them to let them live" (Josh. 9:14-15). Now Israel was operating in open disobedience to the will of God. In this particular case the mistake was costly.

Within three days the Israelites discovered that the Gibeonites were, in fact, their neighbors. But, bound by their word, they were committed to provide for their safety. The Israelites were determined that the Gibeonites would be servants, "hewers of wood and drawers of water unto all the congregation" (Josh. 9:21). One might imagine that the Israelites smugly assumed that they had turned a sinful commitment into a beneficial arrangement. Soon they discovered otherwise.

Several of the kings of Canaan, fearful of the power of the Israelites, determined to attack them at their weakest point, the city of Gibeon. At the height of the battle the Gibeonites sent a message to Joshua, camped at Gilgal. "Slack not thy hand from thy servants; come up to us quickly, and save us, and help us: for all the kings of the Amorites that dwell in the mountain are gathered together against us" (Josh. 10:6). When Joshua's soldiers should have been preparing for the systematic conquest of Canaan, they were, instead, marching off to protect a city of slaves.

When we ignore the counsel of God, we will ultimately make a costly commitment to the world. The following are characteristics of such a commitment.

1. It will become the point of Satan's attack. The treaty with Gibeon was Israel's "ochilles' heel." Because Gibeon was a great city the attention of the enemy was directed to it. What a parallel to the Christian who, ignoring the counsel of God, enters into a relationship (job, dating relationship, investment, purchase) which becomes the point of Satan's attack.

A young executive once related that he had taken a position with his company because it "looked so good he couldn't afford to turn it down." There had been no attempt to find the will of God about the situation. "Now," he confessed, "I find myself compromising my convictions to gain a contract. I am failing as a husband, father, and Christian because I am unable to withstand the constant temptation." His commitment to the world had become the point of Satan's attack.

2. It will always be begging for attention. Joshua was assembling his troops and planning strategy at Gilgal when the message came, "Come up to us quickly, and save us!" This was not in the schedule. The commitment had been made and it required faithfulness. It is the same with commitments made to the world.

Once I purchased an automobile because of its known dependability. The Lord subtly reminded me that I should pray and seek his leadership. But how could I go wrong! For a year and a half it seemed that my "dependable" automobile was constantly in the shop—always begging for attention.

Since then I have visited with others who have made similar

commitments whether for work or pleasure. The comments are always the same. "Something unusual has happened which requires my attention." That's to be expected when you make a commitment to the world.

3. It will deplete your resources. Joshua's men routed the army of the Amorites. In the final assessment they had expended an enormous amount of energy and time in a direction other than that originally planned. Commitments to the world always deplete our resources—physically, spiritually, financially, and emotionally. I have known fine Christians who have gone broke trying to strike it rich. Resources which might have been used to win many to Christ were dissipated.

The prophet Haggai said of those who ignored the counsel of God, "Consider your ways. Ye have sown much, and bring in little; ye eat, but ye have not enough; ye drink, but ye are not filled with drink; ye clothe yourselves, but there is none warm; and he that earns wages earns wages to put it into a bag with holes" (Hag. 1:5-6). What an appropriate word for us. Consider your ways! Examine your commitments. Is it possible that your resources are being depleted by a commitment to the world?

It is unfortunate that we are prone to walk by sight rather than faith. We believe what we perceive with our physical senses, more readily than that which the Lord reveals through his Word. The result is a history of commitments made to the world. We lose the freedom that comes from acting on the truth of God. Are you involved in such a commitment at this present time. Is there a way of victory and restored effectiveness?

Joshua discovered that a commitment made to the world must be given to God if victory is ever to be gained. By making servants of the Gibeonites, the Israelites thought they had turned bad to good. Their attempt, however, resulted in the added obligation of protecting those who were actually their enemies. They soon discovered that only God can make "all things work together for good to them that love [Him], to them who are the called according to his purpose" (Rom. 8:28).

As Joshua marched his troops from Gilgal to Gibeon the Lord spoke to him. This time Joshua listened and obeyed. "And the Lord said unto Joshua, Fear them not; for I have delivered them into thine hand. There shall not a man of them stand before thee. Joshua *therefore*, came unto them suddenly, and went up from Gilgal all night" (Josh. 10:8-9). It was on this occasion that the Lord performed one of the greatest miracles in history. God caused the sun and moon to stand still at the command of Joshua. "And there was no day like that before it or after it, that the Lord hearkened unto the voice of a man: for the Lord fought for Israel" (Josh. 10:14). There followed the successful campaign that allowed all the southern portion of Canaan to be taken by the Israelites.

There is a simple, but important lesson to be learned here: If you have made a commitment to the world because you ignored the counsel of God, turn to God now and seek a word regarding the proper behavior for victory. Do what you failed to do at first. It might be that God's method of deliverance will be recorded as one of the greatest miracles of your life!

8
Why Prayers Are Hindered

Many Christians have given up on the possibility of entering into an effective prayer ministry. They are quick to agree that prayer changes things, but must confess that very little, if anything, seems to happen when they pray. Some have turned to prayer during a great crisis and suffered disappointment. Others have asked for guidance at critical times but apparently never heard from the Lord. They would hesitate to discount the significance of prayer but have long since discarded the possibility of its practical usefulness in their lives.

Why were their prayers hindered? Did they pray incorrectly? Were they simply ignorant of the answer when it did come? Was some important quality missing in their lives? Did they overlook some cardinal principle of prayer? Is it possible that prayer is simply not intended to be an effective ministry for them? I have heard individuals offer these and other reasons for their failure to pray effectively.

In this chapter we will examine the hindrances to prayer. It must be understood that prayer is both the privilege and the responsibility of every Christian. Our Lord said that "men ought always to pray and not to faint" (Luke 18:1). Since we are commanded to pray it follows that every Christian can pray effectively. If your prayer life is faltering it may be for one of the following reasons.

Neglect of Personal Holiness

It is significant that we will never sway God by personal righteousness. Our righteousness is found in Christ. This is the meaning of praying "in Jesus' name." We are coming to God on the basis of what Christ has done and is doing in our lives. Hebrews 4:14-16 reminds us that since "we have a great high priest, that is passed into the heavens, . . . let us hold fast our profession. For we have not an high priest who cannot be touched with the feeling of our infirmities, but was in all points tempted like as we are, yet without sin. Let us, therefore, come boldly unto the throne of grace, that we may obtain mercy, and find grace to help in time of need." In other words our authority to approach God in prayer is based entirely on the work of Christ which makes us acceptable to God.

On the other hand, we must acknowledge that persistent sin on the part of the believer strikes at the heart of effective prayer. "Who shall ascend into the hill of the Lord?" asks the psalmist. "Or who shall stand in his holy place? He that hath clean hands, and a pure heart; who has not lifted up his soul unto vanity, nor sworn deceitfully" (Ps. 24:3-4). A failure to concentrate on personal holiness shows an arrogant disregard for the work of Christ. Additionally, it places in Satan's hands the necessary tool to play out his role of accuser.

How often have you undertaken to pray only to be reminded of your personal failure in the area of purity. "How can I ask God to deliver me from this crisis?" laments the Christian. "I have been away from him for such a long time." It is tragic that when trouble strikes we often must spend time getting our lives ready to pray, instead of praying.

Believers are especially prone to the sins of presumption. This happens when you presume on the love and grace of God and dare to commit sin. "God is loving," you say, "and since I am a Christian, he must forgive me of this sin. Therefore, I will commit it and settle with God later on." This reasoning is regularly employed by the Christian with habitual sins. Habitual sin is planned upon the assumption that God must forgive. It hardens the heart of the believer making him insensitive to the voice of God.

No wonder the psalmist cried, "Keep back thy servant also from presumptuous sins; let them not have dominion over me" (Ps. 19:13).

Jesus made it clear that we have not repented of any sin we are still committing. Repentance involves a change of mind with a resultant change of action. How can a believer who is insensitive to Christ's death expect to be sensitive to the revealed will of God about other matters? "Create in me a clean heart," beseeched David, and "then will I teach transgressors thy ways; and sinners shall be converted unto thee" (Ps. 51:10,13). James reminds us that, "The effectual, fervent prayer of a righteous man availeth much" (Jas. 5:16).

Praying Out of the Wrong Motive

Many times our prayers are hindered because our motives are impure. "Ye ask, and receive not," states James, "because you ask amiss, that you may consume it upon your lusts" (Jas. 4:3). In other words, your purpose in prayer might be to satisfy a desire of the flesh without any regard to God's will or spiritual welfare. You may be asking God for nothing more than a fulfillment of a personal desire.

Psalm 37:4 is an encouragement to "Delight thyself also in the Lord; and he shall give thee the desires of thine heart." Often our desire is for the gift rather than the Giver. For instance, consider a teenager who has just become old enough for driver's license. His heart's desire is for an automobile of his own. He knows his parents must offer a cosignature for such a purchase. When he approaches them he is reminded of the various indications of his immaturity: Poor grades; disrespect for authority; personal sloppiness; failure to assume responsibilities in the home. His parents tell him that these items must be rectified before any consideration will be given to the purchase of an automobile.

It is amazing how such a remarkable change can occur overnight in the young man's life. His room is clean, his parents are treated with the utmost respect, there is an element of neatness in his personal appearance, and, wonder of wonders, his grades show drastic improvement. Impressed with his mature response and thrilled with his attitude toward them, his parents make possible the purchase of an automobile. He immediately slips back into his old habits. His grades go down; his room is a pigpen; he is never home on time; and his appearance is dismaying. It is obvious that he was delighting himself in the promised automobile, and not his parents.

Frequently Christians try to buy God's favor with good behavior in order to get him to give them what they want. We sometimes even attach exaggerated claims of useful spiritual purpose to that for which we are praying. "Lord, give me the new home and I will entertain lost friends in it." "Lord, get me a raise and I will give more." "Help me get the position and I will use it as a means of testimony." God knows our hearts. He knows whether we are delighting ourselves in him or in the things we want from him.

Several years ago my wife and I were discussing Psalm 37:4. I asked her to list the desires of her heart at that moment. Since we had just moved into a new home, I asked specifically regarding some furniture that was needed. She said we needed a couch that would make into a bed in order to have sleeping arrangements for company. In addition, we needed a large dining table so we could accommodate more people at mealtimes.

We made note of these "desires" and turned our attention to "delighting in the Lord." We even asked him to change the desires if they were not in accord with his will. On Thursday of the same week, our new neighbors visited us. In the course of conversation, they mentioned a "hide-a-bed" sofa they had no place for in their new home. "Would you be interested in purchasing it?" he asked, not knowing the direction of our prayers. "No," I said, and although I did not tell him, the reason was simple—we had no money to make such a purchase. "At least come look at it" he insisted. The next day I made my way to his home to see it. Imagine my surprise when he met me at the door with this statement, "Tom, God told me to give you this sofa!" Needless to say, I was flabbergasted, and after some protest he reminded me that I should allow him to obey God. That morning we moved the sofa to our home, where it fit beautifully.

At noon, the same day, our first guests arrived. Before taking off their coats, they remarked that they had received a substantial Christmas bonus and wanted to purchase something for our home, preferably a new dining table! In short order, the sofa was in the den, the table was in the dining room, and we were, indeed, delighting ourselves in the Lord and his goodness.

I do not mean to infer that we should spend the bulk of our time praying about "things" rather than for people. On the other hand, it must be remembered that God is interested in what concerns us. If we will be interested in what concerns him, he will answer our prayers.

Prayers Hindered By Improper Relationships

Jesus constantly emphasized the importance of being properly related to others—both as a manifestation of our relationship to God and so that we can have confidence in prayer. "And when you stand praying, forgive, if you have aught against any; that your Father also, which is in heaven may forgive you your trespasses. But if you do not forgive, neither will your Father which is in heaven forgive your trespasses" (Mark 11:25-26). Again he said, "Therefore if thou bring thy gift to the altar, and there rememberest that thy brother hath aught against thee; Leave there thy gift before the altar and go thy way; first be reconciled to thy brother, and then come and offer thy gift" (Matt. 5:23-24). The Lord is saying that we are to forgive and to seek the forgiveness of others.

It is impossible for a Christian to have an effective prayer life while either harboring an unforgiving spirit or refusing to seek reconciliation with someone he has wronged. God is interested in drawing men into fellowship with himself. Yet so often we seek the benefits of such a fellowship while at the same time abusing our relationships with others whom he also loves.

Of particular importance is proper conduct toward family members. In 1 Peter 3:7, for instance, husbands are exhorted to dwell with their wives "according to knowledge, giving honour unto the wife, as unto the weaker vessel, and as being heirs together of the grace of life; *that your prayers be not hindered.*" When there is a strain in the family relationship because of improper conduct on the part of believers, every attempt should be made toward reconciliation. Many individuals are called into the ministry of intercession, but family strife hinders their effectiveness. If you cannot pray *with* fellow believers, it is difficult to imagine that you can pray effectively *for* others.

Looking to the Wrong Source of Supply

Christians are notorious for praying to God about a need, while trusting other people to answer that need. Sometimes we even "instruct" God as to who or what is best suited to supply the answer to a specific need. On other occasions, we use subtle devices to inform those we think might meet our need, that we are "believing God" for an answer to prayer.

It is imperative to understand that God is his source of supply. The apostle Paul reminded the Christians in Philippi to "Be careful for nothing, but in every thing by prayer and supplication with thanksgiving let your requests be made known unto God. My God shall supply all your need according to his riches in glory by Christ Jesus" (Phil. 4:6,19).

George Mueller of Bristol, England, is an outstanding example of trusting God alone as the source of supply. Faced with overwhelming needs as he cared for hundreds of orphans, he recalled Abraham's experience when asked to sacrifice his son. God had provided a ram to be sacrificed instead of Isaac. Abraham responded by calling the place "Jehovah-jireh" (Gen. 22:14) or "The Lord will provide."

Mueller determined that he would share the needs of his ministry with God alone, never with other men. His carefully recorded "chronicles" indicate that God never failed to supply what was needed. Often that supply would be delivered in the most unlikely manner as an evidence that God alone was the source of supply.

It is a testimony of our lack of faith when we speak to other men about our needs before speaking to God. We often make every attempt to find an answer before getting "down to trusting God." It cannot be overemphasized: God alone is the Christian's source of supply. Failure to recognize this key fact will result in prayer that is hindered.

Satanic Opposition

To engage in prayer is to enter the arena of spiritual warfare. We are reminded in the sixth chapter of Ephesians that "we wrestle not against flesh and blood, but against principalities, against powers, against the rulers of the darkness of this world, against wickedness in the [atmosphere]" (v. 12). For this reason Paul encourages us to, "Put on the whole armour of God" (v. 11). That the armor is for the person who is "Praying always with all prayer and supplication in the Spirit" (v. 18).

Daniel experienced a delayed answer to prayer because of satanic opposition. After spending many days in prayer asking for God's mercy to be shown to rebellious Israel, he was approached by a heavenly messenger who said, "Fear not, Daniel: for from the first day that thou didst set thine heart to understand, and to chasten thyself before thy God, thy words were heard, and I am come for thy words. But the prince of the kingdom of Persia withstood me one and twenty days: but, lo, Michael, one of the chief princes, came to help me; and I remained there with the kings of Persia" (Dan. 10:12-13). From Daniel's experience we get a glimpse of the warfare that rages between the forces of heaven and hell when a Christian prays.

When you see the warfare which surrounds your prayers, you should put on the armor of God and exercise your authority by praying (1) in the name of Jesus (i.e., based on your position in Christ); (2) because of the shed blood of Jesus (representing Satan's defeat); and (3) on the basis of God's revealed will (what God has spoken to your heart through his Word). Remember that "greater is he that is in you, than he that is in the world" (1 John 4:4).

Divine Purpose

God often waits to answer our prayers so that his glory and power can be more fully manifested. The eleventh chapter of John tells that Jesus waited to respond to the pleas of Mary and Martha for their brother Lazarus until it was obvious that only a miracle of God would suffice. Standing before the tomb of Lazarus, he acknowledged the importance of the moment "because of the people which stand by that they may believe that thou hast sent me" (John 11:42).

Before his ascension Jesus commanded his followers to return to Jerusalem and "wait for the promise of the Father" (Acts 1:4). They gathered in the upper room, praying until the day of Pentecost was fully come. God delayed the answer to their prayers until such a time that worldwide attention would be drawn to the outpouring of his Spirit.

Many days separated God's promise of a son for Abraham and Sarah from the fulfillment of that promise. It was only after all self-effort failed, and bearing a child was an impossibility, that "the Lord did unto Sarah as he had spoken. For Sarah conceived, and bore Abraham a son in his old age, at the set time of which God had spoken to him" (Gen. 21:1-2).

The Scripture abounds with exhortations to "wait upon the Lord." Christians, instead of becoming impatient, should welcome the opportunity to engage in a discipline that will focus attention on the Lord and develop character in the believer. James reminds us that we should not seek the easy out, but "count it all joy when ye fall into divers temptations; Knowing this, that the trying of your faith worketh patience. But let patience have her perfect work that you may be perfect and entire, wanting nothing" (Jas. 1:2-4).

Praying Yourself Out of Faith

"Commit thy way unto the Lord," wrote the psalmist, "trust also in him; and he shall bring it to pass" (Ps. 37:5). In other words, "Give it to him, leave it with him, because he works." Most Christians need that admonition. It is strange that while we bring our burden to the Lord in prayer, we generally do not leave it there. It is apparent that we don't deem him capable of handling most situations. Our prayers seem to take form of reminders (as if God had forgotten) or critical status reports (as if he did not know how things were progressing). It is possible, you know, to pray yourself out of the position of faith. Let me illustrate:

Imagine that you are facing surgery of a very critical nature. Fortunately you are in the best of hospitals and under the care of a surgeon reknown for his expertise in the area of your concern. On the day before the surgery your doctor stops by for a visit. "Doctor," you exclaim, "I am so glad that you are on the case. I have complete confidence in your ability. I have no fear whatsoever that things will turn out any way except the best. I trust you completely and really look forward to getting this situation remedied." The doctor is gratified with your comments and pleased with your confidence. Your calm assurance is going to make his job much easier. A few moments after he leaves, however, you send a nurse scurrying after him. He returns to your room to hear you say, "I really mean it! I really do trust you!"

Later, on the evening before the surgery, some of your friends drop by for a visit. When you express your relief about having the best possible physician, they respond by reminding you of others who've said the same only to meet with great difficulties. Some of them even begin to brag on another surgeon who did such a good job on an acquaintance. After they leave, you quickly dial your doctor to say, "You know I really do trust you because I know you are the best. By the way, I have heard of another doctor who does surgery similar to this. Do you know him?" Your surgeon begins to wonder if you really do trust him.

You are wondering yourself! Late at night you place another call to your doctor. "You know my life is going to be in your hands tomorrow," you say. "I am just checking to see if you are aware of that." When he responds in the affirmative, you ask if he has performed this surgery as often as the other doctor you mentioned earlier. Since he is not sure, you make this final request, "How about having him in the operating room with you!" you blurt out. Your surgeon wisely perceives that, with your confidence at an all-time low and your blood pressure skyrocketing, you are in no position to have surgery tomorrow. He is not sure he wants to perform surgery on a person who doesn't have confidence in him.

We are to pray without ceasing until God gives us a revelation of his will. Once you have his word it is a simple matter of agreeing with it and acting on it.

The Proper Response

Hindrances to prayer can be grouped in three broad categories: (1) Personal sin; (2) Satanic opposition; and (3) Divine purpose. When our prayers are hindered, we should not be discouraged. Instead, we should seek out the reason and deal with it on biblical terms.

Personal sin must be acknowledged and confessed with a spirit of repentance. First John 1:9 assures us that "If we confess our sins, he is faithful and just to forgive us our sins, and to cleanse us from all unrighteousness." What a great promise to the Christian who has allowed a great barrier of unconfessed sin to obstruct fellowship with the Father.

Satanic opposition is an indication that your prayers are dealing death blows to the devil's army. Revelation 12:11 gives a critical insight into the Christian's tools for spiritual warfare. "And they overcame him [Satan] by the blood of the Lamb, and by the word of their testimony; and they loved not their lives unto the death." Using the authority that is ours because of our position in Christ it is essential that we continue to storm the gates of hell and bind the "strong man" (Matt. 12:29).

Prayer answers delayed by divine purpose should be welcomed as opportunities to express servitude to a sovereign God. We must resist the temptation to take matters in our own hands or quit the matter altogether. We must submit to God's discipline if we are to grow stronger in faith for intercession. The prophet Jeremiah, facing severe persecution, asked the Lord to "hurry up and do something" (Jer. 12:1-4). God's reply indicated that even greater days of testing lay ahead. "If thou hast run with the footmen, and they have wearied thee, then how canst thou contend with horses? and if in the land of peace, wherein thou trustedst, they wearied thee, then how wilt thou do in the swelling of Jordan" (Jer. 12:5). The psalmist reminds us to "Rest in the Lord, and wait patiently for him" (Ps. 37:7).

Since the answer to our prayers rarely comes according to our schedule, it is important to respond properly during the period of delay. Remember that hindered prayer is one more problem acknowledged by a sovereign God. As such it is an indication that he has not given up the possibility we might learn how to pray.

9
Praying for a Blessing

Frequently we punctuate our prayers with the request that God "bless" someone or something. What is meant by such a request? Are we simply asking God to do something good or make something work out all right? Is there a deeper significance to this request which, if understood, would add new earnestness to our praying?

In the biblical sense, a "blessing" is an act of God by which he causes someone or something to supernaturally produce more than would be naturally possible. When you ask the Lord, for instance, to bless a certain missionary, you are asking God to give him the ability to accomplish more than is humanly possible. Praying that God bless an offering indicates a desire for God to superintend the use of that money so that it accomplishes more than it would if dispensed on the basis of human cleverness. A prisoner of war might ask God to bless meager rations so that life could be sustained on a diet which is totally inadequate. God's blessing on a preacher or sermon results in an effective ministry which cannot be explained on the basis of human logic or talents.

Living below the standards of God's blessing shows the world nothing which cannot be attained by human effort. We must have the blessing of God on our lives, our homes, our jobs, churches, and ministries, if the world is to see Christ. How can we obtain the blessing of God? The principles of praying for a blessing are seen in the miracle of feeding the five thousand with five loaves and two fishes as recorded in Matthew 14:15-21. "And when it was evening, his disciples came to him, saying, This is a desert place, and the time is now past; send the multitude away, that they may go into the villages, and buy themselves victuals. But Jesus said unto them, They need not depart; give them to eat. And they say unto him, We have here but five loaves, and two fishes. He said, Bring them hither to me. And he commanded the multitude to sit down on the grass, and took the five loaves, and the two fishes, and looking up to heaven, he blessed, and brake, and gave the loaves to his disciples, and the disciples to the multitude. And they did all eat, and were filled: and they took up the fragments that remained twelve baskets full. And they that had eaten were about five thousand men, beside women and children."

Several facts are evident in this remarkable experience:

1. God's blessing is not limited by the size of your need. Imagine the prospect! A late hour, a deserted place, and over five thousand people are needing to be fed. The disciples, overwhelmed with the magnitude of such a responsibility, request that Jesus "Send the multitude away, that they may go into the villages and buy themselves food" (Matt. 14:15). Jesus is determined to prove that there is no limit to that which may be accomplished when you have the blessing of God.

It is interesting how often we view situations as either too large for our faith, or too small for God's concern. Frankly, Satan has never said to me regarding any issue, "Now that's just the right size for God to handle." He would like to make us think that, before approaching God, we should determine if the solution to a problem is within the realm of possibility.

When Abraham met with the Lord in the plains of Mamre he was given this message, "I will certainly return unto thee according to the time of life; and, lo, Sarah, the wife, shall have a son . . . . Now Abraham and Sarah were old and well stricken in age; and it ceased to be with Sarah after the manner of women. Therefore Sarah laughed within herself, saying, After I have waxed old shall I have pleasure, my lord being old also? And the Lord said unto Abraham, Wherefore did Sarah laugh, saying, Shall I of a surety bear a child, which am old? Is any thing too hard for the Lord?" (Gen. 18:10-14).

Why was Sarah so astounded by the message from the Lord? The Lord had told Abraham on a previous occasion "And I will bless her, and give thee a son also of her" (Gen. 17:16). Like us, she was reluctant to claim that blessing in the face of seemingly insurmountable odds. God's blessing is not limited by the size of your need. "Is anything too hard for the Lord?"

2. God's blessing is not limited by the cause of your need. The disciples urged Jesus to send the people away so that they might buy themselves food. Jesus said unto them "They need not depart; give them to eat" (Matt. 14:16).

It would seem that the disciples had been given the responsibility for feeding the multitude, but the situation had slipped up on them. A desperate attempt to gather provision resulted in a meager supply. "We have here but five loaves and two fishes" (Matt. 14:17). Is it possible that the predicament was caused by their carelessness? No matter! "Bring them hither to me," said the Lord (Matt. 14:18).

Many people labor under the misconception that prayer only avails in situations beyond their cause or control. "I would ask God to deliver," they say, "except for the fact I caused the problem myself. It is a result of my own rebellion and carelessness." That is precisely when the Lord most delights in our approach to his throne of grace—when we are convicted of the hopelessness of our humanity.

Do you remember Colossians 2:6? "As you have therefore received Christ Jesus the Lord, so walk ye in him." When did you receive Christ? It was when you finally became convinced that you were responsible for your sin and no works of righteousness would avail to save. It was then you turned in faith to Christ and received him as Savior. Do you see the pattern? Our walk with Christ will include a day by day acknowledegment of our failure—and a day by day trust in his grace which is sufficient. Do not be misled to believe that God's blessings are limited by the cause of our need. That would cause you to live in the constant strain of trying to earn a right standing with God so that you might pray.

3. God's blessing is not limited by the human resources available. I can picture the disciples taking Christ aside so that others cannot see their distress or hear their conversation. Jesus had said, "Give them to eat" and their hearts had melted. Circled around the Lord they cast furtive glances first at the crowd and then at one another. "You tell him," they each seemed to be saying. Finally, one of them unwrapped the cloth around a small basket. "We have here but five loaves, and two fishes." Surely this would convince the Lord that the multitude must be sent away.

God's blessing is not limited by the human resources available! What a difficult lesson for us to learn! The growth and ministry of many churches has been impeded by the failure to learn this lesson. How often we seem to make our plans on the basis of what *we* think we *can* do, rather than what *God* had said we *must* do. It would be a great day for the Christian witness, if church leaders and committees would be more occupied with seeking the mind of God, than reviewing the result of past human effort and making decisions accordingly. Can you imagine planning the Israelites' journey from Egyptian bondage on the basis of either the previous year's receipts or a projected wilderness economy?

God is our source of supply. Many Christians fail to ask for God's blessing because they assume it must come through an existing channel. The issue is never what we can do, but rather what we will allow God to do through us. Do not be intimidated when you cannot see just how God will answer your need of blessing. "It is the glory of God to conceal a thing" (Prov. 25:2). "But seek ye first the kingdom of God, and his righteousness"; said our Lord, "and all these things shall be added unto you" (Matt. 6:33).

4. God's blessing can be appropriated. "Bring them hither to me." Jesus had said of the loaves and fish. Shortly afterward they all received sufficient food and there were leftovers to spare. What was the key? Look at Matthew 14:19. "And he commanded the multitude to sit down on the grass, and took the five loaves, and the two fishes, and looking up to heaven, he blessed, and brake, and gave the loaves to his disciples, and the disciples to the multitude."

(1) First Jesus assessed the situation. He had seated the people in an orderly fashion as recorded in Mark 6:39-40. There was no question about the size of the need. He took the loaves and fish so that he would know the present resources on hand to meet the need.

Many people are aware of the need for God's blessing but they have never taken the time to accurately assess the situation. It is interesting to note that many of those who are recorded as being mighty in prayer (Mueller, Taylor, Brainerd, etc.) kept careful records of their needs and God's response. This enabled them to see the small amounts as being as much a blessing as the larger amounts.

(2) Jesus sought the mind of God. He looked to heaven—recognizing God as the source of supply and indicating a willingness to conform to the Father's revealed will.

Again the Christian can respond accordingly by seeking a word from God—not only in regard to God's willingness to bless, but also in the manner of behavior which would allow God to bless. At Meribah God assured Moses of his desire to provide water for the Israelites. He also shared with Moses a word regarding his behavior. "Speak ye unto the rock before their eyes; and it shall give forth his water, and thou shalt bring forth to them water out of the rock" (Num. 20:8). Moses acknowledged God's desire to bless, but was not willing to conform to his prescribed pattern of behavior. It was that act which cost Moses his entrance into Canaan.

God could have provided for the multitude in many ways. It was his desire for Christ to divide the loaves and fish. In like fashion as Christ we must seek the mind of God and act accordingly.

(3) He blessed God and requested a blessing on the loaves and fish. In the original language of the New Testament the word for "blessing" indicates an act of praise, consecration, and petition. In this passage we read simply "he blessed." We may assume this blessing included praise to the Father and a request that the loaves and fish be consecrated to his use so that they would provide sufficient food for the multitude.

As we pray for God's blessing, our prayers should similarly include the elements of praise, consecration, and petition. We are asking God to cause someone or something to accomplish in a supernatural fashion more than would be naturally possible. Praising him builds our faith. Consecration settles the issue of lordship and opens the door for making an effective petition.

(4) He acted in obedience to the Father. After the blessing, Jesus "broke and gave the loaves to his disciples and the disciples to the multitude." He not only asked for the blessing, but was also actively involved in its provision.

Many Christians ask the Lord to bless certain individuals or activities but they are not sensitive to the fact God may want them to be the channel of blessing. It is one thing, for instance, to ask God to "bless a missionary." It is another matter to say, "Lord reveal to me how I may be the channel of your blessing and I will act accordingly." The blessed food still required dispensing. Asking God to bless an evangelistic crusade still requires a personal sharing of the gospel. If we are to see God's intended blessing become a reality, we must act in faith according to his revealed will.

Twelve baskets full remaining! How desperately the world needs to see God's blessing on his work in that fashion. Think of it the next time you pray for a blessing.

10
A Missionary's Method of Effective Prayer

During the early years of this century, the Lisu tribespeople in southwest China experienced a remarkable movement of God. Many among the thousands who came to Christ were borne into the presence of God by the prayers and work of Mr. J. O. Fraser, a missionary of the Overseas Missionary Fellowship, formerly called the China Inland Mission.

Mr. Fraser, as Hudson Taylor before him, saw that the success of his missionary work rested on the prayer support of those in his homeland, England. In a letter written to encourage their continued prayers, he suggested that the "prayer of faith" follows certain guidelines. The letter, printed here, will serve to emphasize and amplify the principles shared in the preceding chapters.

TANTSAH, YUNNAN, CHINA
OCTOBER 9, 1915

MY DEAR FRIENDS:

The Scriptures speak of several kinds of prayer. There is intercession and there is supplication; there is labor in prayer and there is the prayer of faith; all perhaps the same fundamentally, but they present various aspects of this great and wonderful theme. It would not be unprofitable to study the differences between these various scriptural terms.

There is a distinction between *general* prayer and *definite* prayer. By definite prayer I mean prayer after the pattern of Matthew 21:21-22 and John 15:7, where a definite petition is offered up and definite faith exercised for its fulfillment. Now faith must be in exercise in the other kind of prayer also, when we pray for many and varied things without knowing the will of God in every case.

In *general prayer* I am limited by my ignorance. But this kind of prayer is the duty of us all (1 Tim. 2:1-2), however vague it has to be. I may know very little, in detail, about the object of my prayer, but I can at any rate commend it to God and leave it all with Him. It is good and right to pray, vaguely, for all people, all lands, all things, at all times.

But *definite prayer* is a very different matter. It is in a special sense "the prayer of faith." A definite request is made in definite faith for a definite answer.

Take the case of a Canadian immigrant as an illustration of the prayer of faith. Allured by the prospect of "golden grain" he leaves home for the Canadian West. He has a definite object in view. He knows very well what he is going for, and that is wheat. He thinks of the good crops he will reap and of the money they will bring him—much like the child of God who sets out to pray the prayer of faith. He has his definite object too. It may be the conversion of a son or daughter; it may be power in Christian service; it may be guidance in a perplexing situation, or a hundred and one other things—but it is definite. Consider the points of resemblance between the cases of the prospective Canadian farmer and the believing Christian:

1. *The breadth of the territory.* Think of the unlimited scope for the farmer in Canada. There are literally millions of acres waiting to be cultivated. No need, there, to tread on other people's toes! Room for all—vast tracts of unoccupied land just going to waste, and good land too. And so it is with us, surely. There is a vast, vast field for us to go up and claim in faith. There is enough sin, enough sorrow, enough of the blighting influence of Satan in the world to absorb all our prayers of faith, and a hundred times as many more. "There remaineth yet very much land to be possessed."

2. *The government encourages immigration.* Think also of the efforts of the Canadian government to encourage immigration. All the unoccu-

pied land belongs to it, but settlers are so badly needed that they are offered every inducement—immigration offices established, sea passages and railway fares reduced, and grants of land made free! And God is no less urgently inviting His people to pray the prayer of faith: *"Ask-ask-ask,"* He is continually saying to us. He offers His inducement too: "Ask, and ye shall receive, that your joy may be full." All the unoccupied territory of faith belongs to Him. And he bids us to come and occupy freely. "How long are ye slack to go in to possess the land?"

3. *There are fixed limits.* Yet this aspect of the truth must not be overemphasized. Blessed fact though it be that the land is so broad, it can easily be magnified out of due proportion. The important thing is not the vastness of the territory but how much of it is actually assigned to us. The Canadian government will make a grant of 160 acres to the farmer-immigrant, and no more. Why no more? Because they know very well he cannot work any more. If they were to give him 160 square miles instead of 160 acres he would not know what to do with it all. So they wisely limit him to an amount of land equal to his resources.

And it is much the same with us when praying the prayer of definite faith. The very word "definite" means "with fixed limits." We are often exhorted, and with reason, to ask great things of God. Yet there is a balance in all things, and we may go too far in this direction. It is possible to bite off, in prayer, more than we can chew. There is a principle underlying II Corinthians 10:13 which may apply to this very matter: "According to the measure of the province [limit] which God apportioned to us as a measure" (A.S.V.). Faith is like muscle, which grows stronger and stronger with use, rather than rubber, which weakens when it is stretched. Overstrained faith is not pure faith; there is a mixture of the carnal element in it. There is no strain in the "rest of faith." It asks for definite blessing as God may lead. It does not hold back through carnal timidity, nor press ahead too far through carnal eagerness.

I have definitely asked the Lord for several hundred families of Lisu believers. There are upward of two thousand Lisu families in the Tantsah district. It might be said, "Why do you not ask for a thousand?" I answer quite frankly, "Because I have not faith for a thousand." I believe the Lord has given me faith for more than one hundred families, but not for a thousand. So I accept the limits the Lord, I believe, has given me. Perhaps God will give me a thousand; perhaps He will lead me to commit myself to this definite prayer of faith later on. This is in accordance with Ephesians 3:20: "above all that we ask or think." But we must not overload faith; we must be sane and practical. Let us not claim too little in faith, but let us not claim too much either. Remember the Canadian immigrant's 160 acres. Consider, too, how the Dominion Government exercises authority in the matter of location. The government has a say as to the *where* as well as the *how much* of the immigrant's claim. He is not invited to wander all over the prairie at his own sweet will and elect to settle down in any place he chooses. Even in regard to the position of his farm he must consult the government.

Do we always do this in our prayers and claims? Do we consult the heavenly government at the outset, or do we pray the first thing that comes to mind? Do we spend time waiting upon God to know His will before attempting to embark on His promises? That this is a principle upon which God works He has informed us very plainly in 1 John 5:14-15. I cannot but feel that this is one cause for many unanswered prayers. James 4:3 has a broad application, and we need to search our hearts in its light. Unanswered prayers have taught me to seek the Lord's will instead of my own. I suppose most of us have had such experiences. We have prayed and prayed and prayed, and no answer has come. The heavens above us have been as brass. Yea, blessed brass, if it has taught us to sink a little more of this ever-present self of ours into the cross of Christ. Sometimes our petition has been such a good one, to all appearances, but that does not insure its being of God. Many "good desires" proceed from our uncrucified selves. Scripture and experience agree that those who live nearest to God are the most likely to know His will. We are called to be "filled with the knowledge of His will" (Col. 1:9). We need to know more of the fellowship of Christ's death. We need to feed on the Word of God more than we do. We need more holiness, more prayer. We shall not, then be in such danger of mistaking His will.

The wonderful promise of John 15:7 is prefixed by a far-reaching "if." I wonder if that verse might not be paraphrased: "If ye abide *not* in me, and my words abide *not* in you, *do not* ask whatsoever ye will, for it shall *not* be done unto you." Perhaps if we examined ourselves more thoroughly before God we might even discover, in some cases, that the whole course of our life was not in accordance with His will. What right would a man have, in such a case, to expect his prayers to be answered? But is not this the fact with regard to much "good" Christian work? "Get your work from God" is a good injunction. How often Christian leaders make their own plans, work hard at them, and then earnestly seek God's blessing on them. How much better, as Hudson Taylor felt, to wait on God to know His plans before commencing! Much Christian work seems to have the stamp of the carnal upon it. It may be "good", it may be successful outwardly, but the Shekinah glory is not there. Now all this applies to the prayer of faith. We must have the assurance that we are in the right place, doing the right work. We must be sure that God is leading us, when we enter upon specific prayer.

It does not follow that because a thing is the will of God, He will necessarily lead *you* to pray for it. He may have other burdens for you. We must *get our prayers from God,* and pray to know His will. It may take time. God was dealing with Hudson Taylor for fifteen years before He laid upon him the burden of definite prayer for the foundation of the China Inland Mission. God is not in a hurry. He cannot do things with us until we are trained and ready for them. We may be certain He has further service, further burdens of faith and prayer to give us when we are ready for them.

4. *The claim endorsed.* Turn to the immigrant again. He has come to an agreement with the Canadian government. He falls in with their terms, he accepts their conditions, he agrees to take over the land allotted to him. So he presents his claim at the proper quarter, and it is at once endorsed. Could anything be more simple? Nor need our claim in the presence of God be any less simple. When we once have the deep, calm assurance of His will in the matter, we put in our claim,

just as a child before his father. A simple request and nothing more. No cringing, no beseeching, no tears, no wrestling. No second asking either.

In my case I prayed continually for the Tengyueh Lisu for over four years, asking many times that several hundred families might be turned to God. This was only general prayer, however. God was dealing with me in the meantime. You know how a child is sometimes rebuked by his parents for asking something in a wrong way—perhaps asking rudely. The parent will respond, "Ask me properly!" That is just what God seemed to be saying to me then: "Ask Me properly! You have been asking Me to do this for the last four years without ever really believing I would do it—now ask *in faith*."

I felt the burden *clearly*. I went to my room alone one afternoon and knelt in prayer. I knew that the time had come for the prayer of faith. And then, fully knowing what I was doing and what it might cost me, I definitely committed myself to this petition *in faith*. I cast my burden upon the Lord and rose from my knees with the deep, restful conviction that I had already received the answer. The transaction was done. And since then (nearly a year ago now) I have never had anything but peace and joy (when in touch with God) in holding to the ground already claimed and taken. I have never repeated the request and never will: there is no need. The asking, the taking, and the receiving occupy but a few moments (Mark 11:24). It is a solemn thing to enter into a faith covenant with God. It is binding on both parties. You lift up your hand to God, you definitely ask for and definitely receive His proffered gift—then do not go back on your faith, even if you live to be a hundred.

5. *Get to work.* To return once more to the Canadian farmer. He has put in his claim, the land has been granted, the deed made out and sealed with the official seal. Is that the end then? No, only the beginning!

He has not yet attained his objective. His objective is a harvest of wheat, not a patch of wasteland, and there is a vast difference between the two. The government never promised him sacks of flour all ready for export—only the land which could be made to yield them. Now is the time for him to roll up his sleeves and get to work. He must build his homestead, get his livestock, call in laborers, clear the ground, plow it and sow his seed. The government says to him in effect, "We have granted your claim—now go and work it!"

And this distinction is no less clear in the spiritual realm. God gives us the ground in answer to the prayer if faith, but not the harvest. That must be worked for in cooperation with Him. Faith must be followed up by works, prayer-works. Salvation is of grace, but it must be worked out (Phil. 2:12) if it is to become ours. And the prayer of faith is just the same. It is given to us by free grace, but it will never be ours until we follow it up, work it out. Faith and works must never be divorced, for indolence will reap no harvest in the spiritual world. I think the principle will be found to hold in any case where the prayer of faith is offered, but there is no doubt that it always holds good in cases where the strongholds of Satan are attacked, where the prey is to be wrested from the strong.

Think of the children of Israel under Joshua. God had given them the land of Canaan—given it to them, notice, by free grace—but see how they had to fight when once they commenced actually to take possession!

Satan's tactics seem to be as follows: He will first of all oppose our breaking through to the place of a real, living faith by all means in his power. He detests the prayer of faith, for it is an authoritative "notice to quit." He does not so much mind rambling, carnal prayers, for they do not hurt him much. This is why it is so difficult to attain to a definite faith in God for a definite object. We have often to strive and wrestle in prayer (Eph. 6:10-12) before we attain this quiet, restful faith. And until we break right through and *join hands with God* we have not attained to real faith at all. Faith is a gift of God—if we stop short of it we are using mere fleshly energy or willpower, weapons of no value in this warfare. Once we attain to real faith, however, all the forces of hell are impotent to annul it. What then? They retire and muster their forces on this plot of ground which God has pledged

Himself to give us, and contest every inch of it. The real battle begins when the prayer of faith has been offered. But, praise God, we are on the winning side! Let us read and reread Joshua 10 and never talk about defeat again. Defeat, indeed! No. Victory! Victory! Victory!

Please read II Samuel 23:8-23. All I have been saying is found in a nutshell in verses 11 and 12. Let Shammah represent the Christian warrior. Let David represent the crucified and risen Christ—and note that Shammah was "one of the mighty men that David has." Let the "plot of ground" represent the prayer of faith. Let the lentils, if you will, represent the poor lost souls of men. Let the Philistines represent the hosts of wickedness. Let "the people" represent Christians afflicted with spiritual anemia.

I can imagine what these people were saying as they saw the Philistines approaching and ran away" "Perhaps it was not the Lord's will to grant us that plot of ground. We must submit to the will of God."

Yes, we must indeed submit ourselves to God, but we must also "resist the devil" (James 4:7). The fact that the enemy comes upon us in force is no proof that we are out of the line of God's will. The constant prefixing of "if it be Thy will" to our prayers is often a mere subterfuge of unbelief. True submission to God is not inconsistent with virility and boldness. Notice what Shammah did—simply *held his ground.* He was not seeking more worlds to conquer at that moment. He just stood where he was and hit out, right and left. Notice also the result of his action and to whom the glory is ascribed.

6. *Praying through to victory.* I repeat that this does not necessarily apply to every kind of prayer. A young Lisu Christian here is fond of telling an experience of his a few months ago. He was walking the fields in the evening when his insides began unaccountably to pain him. He dropped on his knees and, bowing his head down to the ground, asked Jesus to cure him. At once the stomachache left him. Praise the Lord! And there are no doubt multitudes of such cases—simple faith and simple answers.

But we must not rest content with such prayer. We must get beyond stomachache or any other ache and enter into the deeper fellowship of God's purposes. "That we henceforth be no more children" (Eph.

4:14). We must press on to maturity. We must attain to "the measure of the stature of the fulness of Christ," and not remain in God's kindergarten indefinitely. If we grow into manhood in the spiritual life we shall not escape conflict. As long as Ephesians 6:10-18 remains in the Bible, we must be prepared for serious warfare—"and having done all, to stand." We must fight through and then stand victorious on the battlefield.

Is not this another secret of many unanswered prayers—that they are not fought through? If the result is not seen as soon as expected, Christians are apt to lose heart and, if it is still longer delayed, to abandon it altogether.

We must count the cost before praying the prayer of faith. We must be willing to pay the price. We must mean business. We must set ourselves to "see things through" (Eph. 6:18, "with all perseverance"). Our natural strength will fail: and herein lies the necessity of a divinely given faith. We can then rest back in the everlasting Arms and renew our strength continually. We can then rest as well as wrestle. In this conflict-prayer, after the definite exercise of faith, there is no need to ask the same thing again and again. It seems to me inconsistent to do so. Under these circumstances, I would say let the prayer take the following forms:

a. A firm standing on God-given ground, and a constant assertion of faith and claiming of victory. It is helpful, I find, to repeat passages of Scripture applicable to the subject. Let faith be continually strengthened and fed from its proper source, the Word of God.

b. A definite fighting and *resisting of Satan's host* in the name of Christ. As direct weapons against Satan, I like to read in prayer such passages as 1 John 3:8: "For this purpose the Son of God was manifested, that he might destroy the works of the devil," and Revelation 12:11: "They overcame him by the blood of the Lamb." I often find it a means of much added strength and liberty to fight in this way. Nothing cuts like the Word of the living God (Heb. 4:12).

c. Praying through every aspect of the matter in detail. In the case of my Lisu work here, I continually pray to God for a fresh knowledge of His will, more wisdom in dealing with the people, knowledge of how to pray, how to maintain the victory, how to instruct the people in the Gospel or in singing or in prayer, help in studying the language, help in ordinary conversation, help in preaching, guidance about choice of a central place to live in, guidance about building a house (if necessary), guidance in my personal affairs (money, food, clothes, etc.), help and blessing in my correspondence, openings for the Word and blessing in other villages, for leaders and helpers to be raised up for me, for each of the Christians by name, also for every one of my prayer helpers by name. Such detailed prayer is exhausting, but I believe effectual in ascertaining the will of God and obtaining His highest blessing.

I would not ask anyone to join me in the definite prayer for the turning to God of several hundred Lisu families unless God gives him individual guidance to do so. Better offer prayer in a more general way than make a definite petition apart from His leading. I should, however, value highly the prayer cooperation of any who feel led to join me in it. What I want, too, is not just an occasional mention of my work and its needs before the Lord, during the morning or evening devotions, but a definite time (say half an hour or so?) set apart for the purpose every day, either during the daytime or in the evening. Can you give that time to me—or rather, to the Lord?

About a fortnight ago I baptized two Lisu women at the little village of Six Family Hollow, the wives of two young Lisu men I baptized last January. I have now baptized six Christian Lisu altogether, all from that one family. It was my painful duty, however, only the next day, to exclude Ah-do from church fellowship. It appears that he has been continually breaking the seventh commandment, not only in his own villages but also in other places where he has been with me. The Lisu are a very immoral race in any case, but in spite of his Christian profession he has been even more promiscuous than most of them. He seems quite penitent and never attempted to deny his guilt. We must pray for his restoration.

I have no other special news of the work just now. I am thinking of visiting Six Family Hollow again in a few days, as well as other villages.

Hoping to write again next month, and with earnest prayers for you all,

Yours in the Lord's service,
J. O. FRASER

Here we find a missionary urgently requesting others to join with him in the practice of prayer. His readers were well aware of the millions of lost souls in China. They didn't need to be reminded that the Scriptures abound with examples and commands to pray. J. O. Fraser outlined the biblical method of prayer because he felt that knowing better "how" to pray would encourage Christians to live up to their responsibility.

J. O. Fraser's effectiveness as a missionary is felt by many to stem from his personal prayer life and from the small prayer groups he encouraged in England.

During the years of Fraser's service among the Lisu people and in the years that followed, tens of thousands of these people came to know Christ. This ministry was multiplied in a marvelous way when some thirty thousand Lisus migrated to Burma where they linked up with Christian churches already established in Burma.

The forty-five thousand Lisus who remained in Southwest China continued to bear witness to Christ in the troubled years that followed.

Then, as now, the world is in desperate need of men and women like J. O. Fraser who will aggressively cooperate with God in his great plan of redemption. Your effectiveness in God's work will depend on how closely you walk with him in prayer.

At the outset of this book, you were asked to consider what has happened to the practice of prayer in your life. Permit the final question: What *is* happening *now* to the practice of prayer in your life? Both heaven and earth are bending to hear your answer.